MACINTOSH
NOTEBOOK

MacPrint

JOHN HEILBORN

Prentice-Hall, Inc., Englewood Cliffs, New Jersey 07632

Library of Congress Cataloging in Publication Data

Heilborn, John
    Macintosh notebook : MacPaint

    Includes index.
    1. Macintosh (Computer)—Programming.
    2. MacPaint (Computer program) 3. Computer
    graphics. I. Title.
    QA76.8.M3H45 1985   001.64'2   84-18359
    ISBN 0-13-542283-3

                    ISBN 0-13-542283-3

This book is available at a special discount when ordered
in bulk quantities. Contact Prentice-Hall, Inc., General
Publishing Division, Special Sales, Englewood Cliffs, N.J. 07632

Bookware® is a registered trademark of Prentice-Hall, Inc.

This book is dedicated to my brother, Jim, and my sister,
Joanne It is easy to forget how important beginnings can
be I remember now

10   9   8   7   6   5   4   3   2   1

Printed in the United States of America

Editorial/production supervision by Lori L. Baronian
Cover design by Hal Siegel
Manufacturing buyer: Frank Grieco

Macintosh is a registered trademark, licensed to Apple Computer

Prentice-Hall International, Inc., *London*
Prentice-Hall of Australia Pty Limited, *Sydney*
Prentice-Hall Canada Inc., *Toronto*
Prentice-Hall Hispanoamericana, S.A., *Mexico*
Prentice-Hall of India Private Limited. *New Delhi*
Prentice-Hall of Japan, Inc., *Tokyo*
Prentice-Hall of Southeast Asia Pte. Ltd., *Singapore*
Whitehall Books Limited, *Wellington, New Zealand*
Editora Prentice-Hall do Brasil Ltda., *Rio de Janeiro*

Contents

INTRODUCTION

Introduction:

This chapter explains how to set up MacPaint and make working copies of the program. It also describes the difference between the original version of MacPaint and the new release.

To begin, turn the page.

[OK]

One of the first things that most people do after setting up Macintosh initially is to insert the MacPaint disk and begin drawing. If you did this, and you followed all of the directions that came with MacPaint, you may still be using the master disk that MacPaint came on. If this is the case and if you have been using MacPaint for a while, you will have almost certainly run into this message:

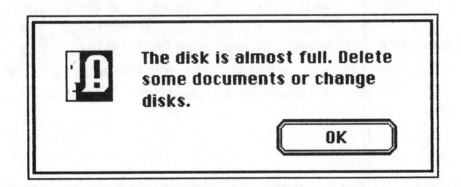

> The disk is almost full. Delete some documents or change disks.
>
> OK

When this message appears, you have no choices (although you might think you do, since it makes two suggestions). You must first click the **OK** (which exits MacPaint). You may then exercise your options, deleting some files or changing disks. Entering <u>anything</u> else will result in an error tone.

Another problem that can occur (and this one is actually more of a disaster than a problem) is what Mac calls a "Serious System Error."

You'll know that you've gotten one of these because you'll be presented with this message:

> ![bomb] **Sorry... A serious system error has occurred. You may choose to restart the system or attempt to resume the current application.**
>
> (Restart)   (Resume)   **ID = 26**

Although you may be able to recover from this kind of error, more often than not you will find that this means you need a new program disk. Unfortunately, if you were using the master disk when this happened, you won't have another disk to run.

Okay, enough with the horror stories. The whole point of this is to motivate you to make at least one back-up disk of MacPaint. That way you'll have lots of space to experiment and you'll still have a copy of MacPaint even if something terrible does happen to the copy you're using.

 # Making Backup Disks

There are several ways that you can make back-up disks. In every case, however, there is one thing that is essential: extra blank disks. If you don't have any on hand, go get some now: I'll wait... ⟵

Now, once you've gotten some blank disks, the next thing you'll need to do is initialize them. That's because the disks that run on the Mac can also be used on different computers and each

By the way, you'll need at least two disks.

of the different computers writes its data somewhat differently onto the disk. Initializing the disk sets up the disk to be used on your computer.

To initialize a new disk, simply put it into the disk drive. Note: If there is a disk already in the disk drive, point the arrow at the menu at the top of the screen that is labeled **File** and pull it down until the word **Eject** is highlighted.

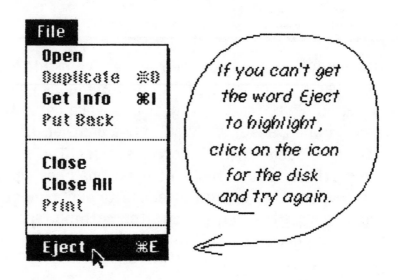

Once you have put the disk into the drive, you will hear some soft whirring noises. This is the computer trying to read what is on the disk. Remember, though, there is nothing on the disk, so after a short while the computer will give up and tell you that the disk is unreadable. It will also ask you if you want to eject it or initialize it.

If you get this message after installing a disk that you believe actually has some data, eject it and re-insert it so the computer will try reading it again.

In this instance, however, click the **Initialize** button.

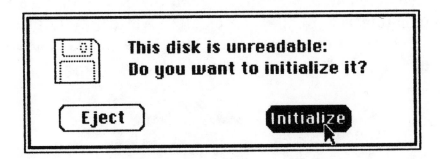

Once again you will hear some soft whirring. This time Mac will initialize the disk. When initialization is complete, the computer will ask you to name the disk.

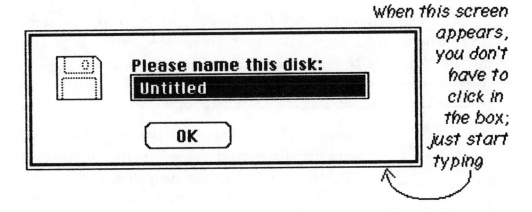

When this screen appears, you don't have to click in the box; just start typing

   If you click the OK button, your disk will be named **Untitled**. Instead, let's call this one: MacPaint Backup. After you have typed the name, pressing the Return key or clicking the **OK** will write the new name on the disk. If you decide to change the name later, all you need to do is select the disk name (with the arrow), backspace to delete the old name, and enter a new one.

After you have named your new disk, the next step is copying everything from the master disk (Write/Paint) to the new disk (MacPaint Backup). Actually, we'll be copying MacWrite and all of the system files also. Anyway, to copy the disk, point the arrow at the icon (picture) of the master disk (Write/Paint), click the button, and hold it down while you "drag" the image of the icon on top of the copy disk icon (MacPaint BackUp).

Notice that the image that is "dragged" over is like a ghost, the actual icon stays where it was

Drag the ghost icon right on top of the icon for the backup disk. When the backup disk's icon turns black, let go of the mouse button. You will then get the following, ominous message:

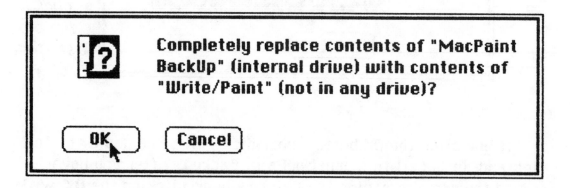

Completely replace contents of "MacPaint BackUp" (internal drive) with contents of "Write/Paint" (not in any drive)?

OK   Cancel

don't worry, this is just Mac's friendly way of telling you that everything on the backup disk will be erased and replaced with the stuff in Write/Paint... go ahead and click "OK".

x

By the way, the messages about the "internal drive" and "not in any drive" are just there to let you know what disks Mac is talking about. If you had an extra drive, Mac would call it the "external drive". Anyway, after you click the OK button, Mac will go off and count the number of programs that need to be copied and will display that number in a small window that looks like this:

Files Remaining to copy | 12 |

The number that appears in the box will decrease as the files are copied.

In addition to the message box that tells you how many files remain to be copied, those of us with only one disk drive (most of us) will get this message:

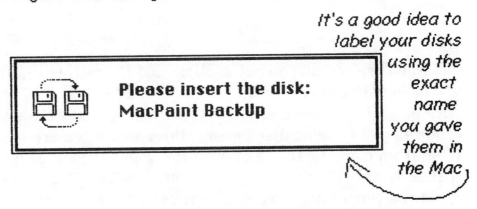

**Please insert the disk:
MacPaint BackUp**

It's a good idea to label your disks using the exact name you gave them in the Mac

In fact, you will get this message numerous times. Each time, Mac will spit out its current disk and ask for another disk by name and wait for you to insert that disk. If you insert the wrong disk, Mac will reject it and repeat the message. Don't worry about keeping track of what disk is where, Mac will take care of all that for you.

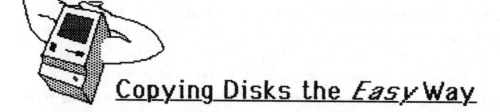

Copying Disks the *Easy* Way

By now, you're probably thinking "There must be an easier way to copy disks"! Changing disks about fifteen or twenty times can get a bit tiresome, so Apple has released a new version of the Macintosh operating system. This disk has a slightly modified MacPaint and a new utility called Disk Copy. To check if you have this program double-click the master disk and look for an icon that looks like this:

Double-clicking means pressing the mouse button twice, quickly

Disk Copy

If you are copying an entire disk, and it has lots of files, and you have only one disk drive (as do most of us), this program can save you a lot of trouble. You see, with only one disk drive, Mac requires you to swap disks many times while you are copying the files from one disk to the other. Disk Copy will copy an entire disk with only four exchanges. If you have Disk Copy, use it to make the second backup disk. We'll call it: Write/Paint Work Disk".

To start the Disk Copy utility, double-click its icon, (point the arrow at the picture of the two disks like the one above and click the mouse button twice, quickly). Once you have done this, the Disk Copy screen will zoom out of its icon and fill the desk top. If this doesn't happen, try again—it takes some practice to double-click reliably.

Whether you use the Disk Copy utility or the older method of copying disks, when you are done, you should have two copies of the MacWrite/MacPaint master disk. For now, put the disk named "Write/Paint Work Disk" away.

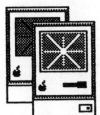

Mac and the Start-Up Disk

Turn the Mac OFF and then ON again. Now insert the disk named "MacPaint Backup." This will become the "start-up" disk. It will be the main disk that Mac will use to find various important files such as the "Scrapbook" and the "clipboard." Note: If you don't know what these are or how to use them, don't worry—don't run back to your Apple manuals to look them up. For the moment they are not important. When you need to use them, we'll look at them in plenty of detail. All you need to know is that we want Mac to use the new disk as its start-up disk. If you don't do this, you may be prompted to insert the master disk (that you put away) in the disk drive. That can be a real pain if you are in the middle of a MacPaint document.

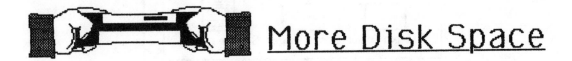 # More Disk Space

Double click the icon for the start-up disk (the only one on the screen... I mean, desk top). You'll find that you have only 47K or 60K, depending on whether you are using the old disk or the new one. This is not good, since you'll need as much as 30K disk space for just one MacPaint document (picture). As you can see, this makes the Write/Paint disk very limiting as it is. Fortunately, there are quite a few files on this disk that we just don't need when we use MacPaint. Also, there are several files that we'll only use occasionally. If we delete those files, we'll have a lot more space to work with.

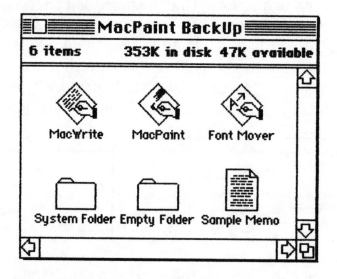

A Closer Look at The System Disk...

Double-click the MacPaint BackUp disk and you will be be able to view the files that it contains. These include: MacWrite, MacPaint, Font Mover, the System Folder, an Empty Folder, and the Sample Memo.

Clearly, we will not be needing all of these on our MacPaint disk. For example, we can remove MacWrite and its Sample Memo without affecting MacPaint at all.

To delete a file, point the arrow at it, press the mouse button and hold it while you "drag" its icon over to the trash can. When the file is in the garbage, the can will turn dark momentarily and the icon for that file will disappear.

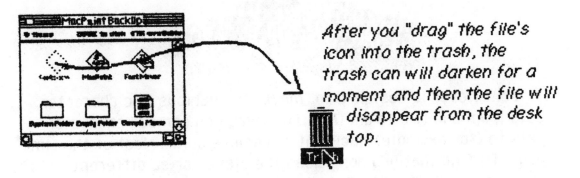

After you "drag" the file's icon into the trash, the trash can will darken for a moment and then the file will disappear from the desk top.

Go ahead and delete both MacWrite and Sample Memo by "dragging" them into the trash. Now look at the amount of memory space left on the disk—it's still just 47K! What happened?

The Mac does not erase files from the disk until you "Empty" the trash. All it does is move the files from one place to another on the desk top. To "Empty" the trash, point the arrow at the menu at the top of the screen named "Special". Pull down the menu and you will see:

Pull the arrow down until the words "Empty Trash" are highlighted and let go of the mouse button. Mac will then "Empty the Trash" and the used memory space will be put back into the disk.

Font Mover is designed to "move" the various Mac character sets from one file to another. That way you can add character sets to (for example) MacPaint or remove some. Most of the time you will find that you don't need the eleven or so different character sets that MacPaint may use. Since the character sets use up lots of disk space, take the time now to look at the styles available and settle on just the two or three that you are likely to want most of the time. The character sets that are standard with the Mac are:

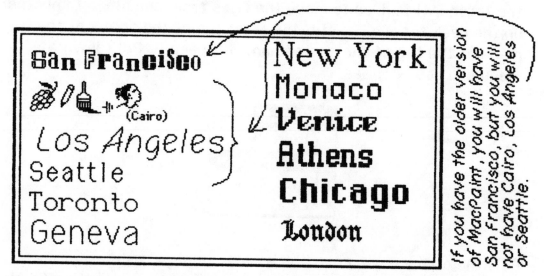

Note: Some of these fonts are necessary for the system to work and you will not be able to remove them. These sets are:

Chicago-12, Geneva-9, Geneva-12 and Monaco-9. The numbers after the name of the font (type style) indicate the size of the characters. The larger the number, the larger the characters. For example, here are all of the available font sizes for Chicago:

9 point ———→ **Chicago**

Chicago ←——— 10 point

12 point ———→ **Chicago**

Chicago ←——— 14 point

18 point ———→ **Chicago**

Chicago ←——— 24 point

36 point —→ **Chicago**

Chicago ←—— 48 point

72 point —→ **Chicago**

Take a close look at these characters. They are all derived from a single character set: Chicago 12. To get the larger and smaller sizes, Mac looks at the 12 point characters and calculates the shapes. Chicago needs only one size of characters in memory because it is a relatively simple character set. Geneva, on the other hand, needs two sets (9 and 12) to produce all nine type sizes cleanly.

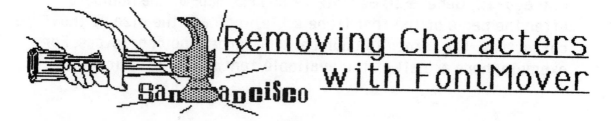

Removing Characters with FontMover

Okay, now it's time to remove the character sets that you will not be using often. For this example, we'll remove Athens from our backup disk. To begin, double-click the Font Mover icon. After a few moments of whirring and buzzing, you should see this screen:

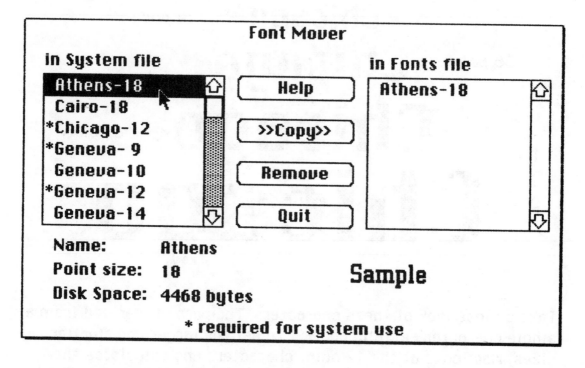

This window tells you the name of each character set, its size, how much memory it uses on the disk and whether it is needed for the Mac to work. It also shows you what the characters look like.

Before you can copy or remove any files, you must select them
by pointing at them with the arrow and clicking the mouse button.
In the illustration on the previous page, we've just clicked the
mouse button and Athens has been highlighted. This also shows a
sample of the type style, its size, etc. You should also notice that
the words **Copy** and **Remove** are now active. When you select a
type style that is on the left side of the control buttons (in the
system file), the arrows around **Copy** will point to the right,
allowing you to copy the file from the system file to the Fonts
file. If you select a type style from the Fonts file, the **Copy**
arrows will point to the left, allowing you to copy that type
style onto the system file.

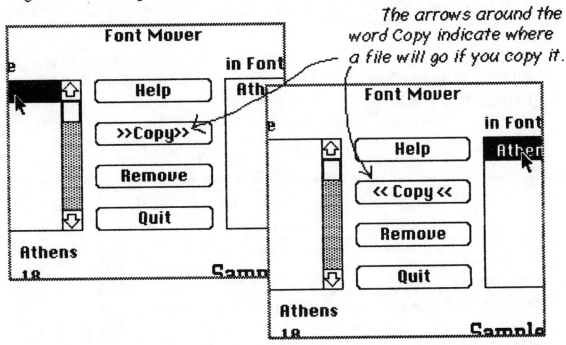

The arrows around the word Copy indicate where a file will go if you copy it.

A word of caution: if you click the **Remove** button and you have
not copied the character set, it will be gone. Of course, you've
got another copy of all the character sets on the master disk, so if
you do make a mistake, you can always get any lost files back by

xix

copying them from the master disk.

Anyway, the procedure that I recommend for removing files is to first copy the file from the system (click the type style from the list on the left side) and put it into the fonts file (just click >> COPY >>). Then click the **Remove** button and it will be deleted from the system file.

Once you have finished moving all of the files that you want to delete over to the fonts file, click on the **Quit** button (point the arrow at Quit and click the mouse button once). The Font Mover screen will disappear and this message will appear:

> **The Font Mover is updating the System and Fonts files. This might take as long as a minute.**

When the Font Mover does finish, the desk top should return and your disk window should now contain a new icon called Fonts. If you don't see Fonts, use one of the scroll arrows to move the inside of the window or use the control box in the lower, right hand corner of the window to make the window larger.

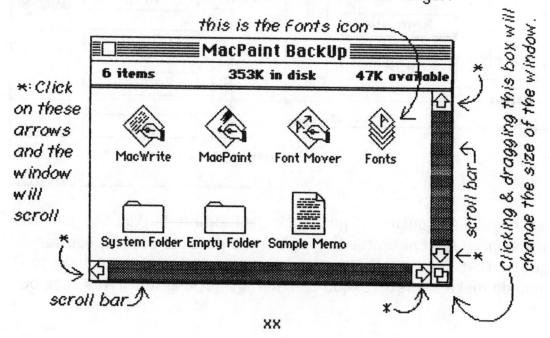

this is the Fonts icon

Clicking & dragging this box will change the size of the window.

*: Click on these arrows and the window will scroll

scroll bar

MacPaint BackUp

6 items   353K in disk   47K available

MacWrite   MacPaint   Font Mover   Fonts

System Folder   Empty Folder   Sample Memo

scroll bar

Note: The scroll arrows (marked by an asterisk on the previous page) will only work if their corresponding scroll bar is gray. If the scroll bar is white, clicking on the arrows will have no effect. ⟵

If the scroll bars are white, the whole screen is visible.

Okay, now that you have created a Fonts file (containing all of the type styles that you want to remove from the MacPaint BackUp disk, you have two options:

1) Delete the Fonts file
2) Save the Fonts file on another disk
   and then delete it from this disk.

Each of these methods has advantages and disadvantages. Let's look at item 1 first. Simply deleting the Fonts file is very easy: just drag the Fonts icon into the trash and the next time you empty the trash, the file will be gone. However, should you later decide that you want one of the deleted type styles, you'll have a bit more work getting the fonts since they'll have to be copied from the master disk.

On the other hand, if you want to save the Fonts file before you remove it from this disk, you'll need to copy it onto another disk... that will require initializing a new disk and going through the copy procedure. Actually, it's a good idea to copy all files unless you are absolutely positive that you won't need them again. It's a bit more trouble—but copies are the best form of insurance.

Any way, if you plan on saving the file first, go back to the section on initializing a disk and then to the section on copying files if you don't remember how those procedures work. When you're done, delete the Fonts file and Font Mover by dragging them into the trash and emptying it.

By the way, it isn't necessary to make another copy of Font Mover since it is very easy to simply copy that directly from the master disk any time you need it.

Old Paint vs New*

*Weighing the differences

As of the writing of this book, there are two versions of Mac-Paint available. The first one (called version 1.0) is the one that was originally released when Macintosh was released. The newer version (called 1.3) was released May 15, 1984. In this section, we'll discuss the differences between the old and new versions and how the differences can affect your pictures, and so on.

New Characters...

The first difference we'll cover is the one we touched upon earlier in this chapter: the character set(s). The old version of MacPaint has a character set called **San Francisco**. As you can see, San Francisco is a mish-mosh of assorted character sizes and styles...and is for the most part a waste of valuable disk space. In the new version of MacPaint, San Francisco has been deleted and three new character sets have taken its place:

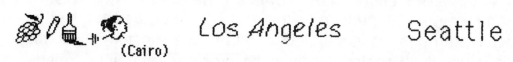
(Cairo)   *Los Angeles*   Seattle

Cairo is a character set that contains modern hieroglyphics such as pencils, cars, paint brushes, and electronic symbols (the complete Cairo character set is shown in Chapter Four: Font on pages 109-110). Los Angeles appears hand-written and Seattle is a non proportional font, similar to Geneva. For more information on character sets, turn to Chapter Four: Fonts).

In addition to the three new character sets, there is a new font size available: 10 point. This was apparently added because of the considerable size difference between 9 point and 12 point characters.

Transparent Paint

The next difference in the new MacPaint is the addition of transparent paints. Ordinarily, if you put one shape or shade over another, the new shape or shading totally covers the old one.

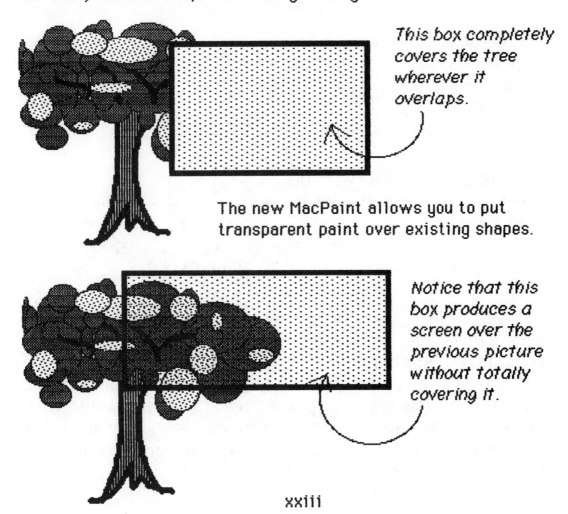

This box completely covers the tree wherever it overlaps.

The new MacPaint allows you to put transparent paint over existing shapes.

Notice that this box produces a screen over the previous picture without totally covering it.

Fill

Up to this point, all of the changes we've discussed in the new MacPaint have been changes to existing commands or features. Fill is a new command that appears in the Edit menu. It can work in two different ways:

1) If you select an area with the Selection Box (⌷), Fill will paint that area with the current pattern. ⟶

2) If you select an area with the Lasso (⌇), Fill will paint the outlined area. ⟶

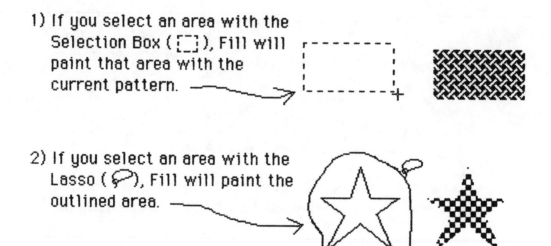

So, if these are so much like two existing commands, why add them to MacPaint? The answer is simple: By providing another way of performing a task, it gives you added flexibilty. For example, let's say you have an existing shape and you only decide to fill it after seeing it. The old version of MacPaint would make you re-draw your picture. With the new version, you simply lasso that shape to select it and then pull down **Fill** from the **Edit** menu at the top of the screen.

If you look along the bottom edge of the screen while you're using MacPaint you will see an assortment of thirty eight (38) different patterns. You can use these to add "color/texture" to MacPaint drawings. The older version of MacPaint had one pattern that has been replaced in the newer version.

this is the old pattern   *and this is the new one*

Since tastes vary, you may find that you prefer the old pattern to the new one. If you want to use the old pattern, just point the arrow at the box that contains the new pattern and double-click the mouse. Mac will respond by presenting this control box:

enlarged image of the current pattern

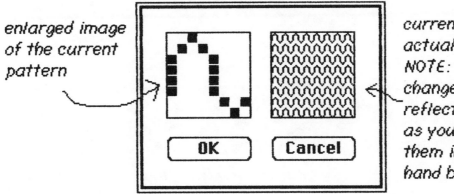

current pattern actual size. NOTE: this changes to reflect changes as you make them in the left-hand box.

This gives you an enlarged image of the new pattern. To put in the old pattern, all you need to do is point the arrow at the dots in the box directly above the OK button. Clicking on a black dot will

xxv

make that dot white and clicking on a white dot will make that dot black. The old pattern looks like this.

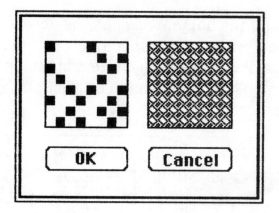

To replace the new pattern with the old one, just copy this pattern into the left box and click the OK button.

For more information on how to use, change, and save these patterns read Chapter One: About Patterns.

CHAPTER ONE

Contents

Chapter One: The Toolbox ...

Along the left side of the MacPaint screen are twenty different icons, each representing a different tool in the MacPaint toolbox. This chapter describes what each does and how they can be used to make MacPaint pictures.

To begin, turn the page...

[OK]

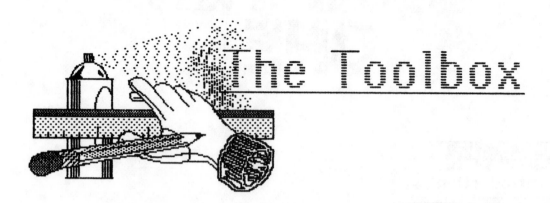

The Toolbox

In this chapter, we'll use all of the MacPaint tools. These are represented by the twenty icons that are displayed vertically along the left side of the screen.

When MacPaint first comes up on the screen, the Paint Brush is enabled

MacPaint is a complete art/drafting studio with an enormous supply of equipment just waiting to be picked up and used.

To pick up a tool, just point the arrow at the tool's icon and click the mouse button once. The icon will then darken and the pointer will change from whatever it was (arrow, etc) to whatever you selected (Paint Brush, Pencil, or whatever).

Now look at the lower left corner of the screen. There is a box there with five different line widths: dotted (no line) and four widths each wider than the last.

In addition to the 38 patterns that are built into MacPaint, you can replace any of the patterns with designs of your own as we discussed in the introduction.

Although it is possible to click and use any of the MacPaint tools at any time, the paint brush is the default MacPaint tool so we'll begin our discussion of the tools with the paint brush.

2

By the way, there are a couple of terms that I used on the last page that may not be familiar to you: enable and default. In fact, throughout this book I may occasionally use terms that are not "standard English." Each time I do this, I will try to explain those terms either right there or at least shortly afterward. Therefore if you spot a strange word from time to time, take a moment to look in the margins. If the definition isn't there then read on a bit further, I'll do my best to explain every word that falls into the category of "Computerese."

Default \dee-folt\

A decision made by the computer on the initial setup of a program. For example, on the previous page, I called the paint brush "the default tool." This means that when MacPaint first appears, it needs to have some tool "ON" and since you can't select a tool until MacPaint has settled down, it needs to make an initial selection for you. For the sake of simplicty, the paint brush is always that tool ... the default tool.

You should be aware that there are numerous default settings that are made for you by not only computers but really any device that can be set in more than one position. Another more common example of this would be your car. When you first put in the key, it must be in the default position (OFF) for the key to be inserted. This is a decision that was built into the car for you when the car was manufactured.

Enable \in-ā-bel\

To turn on a function or set up conditions so that function may be turned on. In the case of the paint brush, these means that the paint brush icon is highlighted (actually darkened) and the current brush shape (also a default setting—made by the computer) is selected to appear as soon as the mouse pointer is positioned in the MacPaint work area.

The Paint Brush

As I just mentioned, the paint brush is the MacPaint tool that is initially set to go when Mac Paint is first turned ON. You'll be able to see this because the paint brush icon will be highlighted in the set of boxes to the left of the work area. All you need to do to use the paint brush is put the mouse pointer in the work area and press down on the mouse button as you move the mouse around.

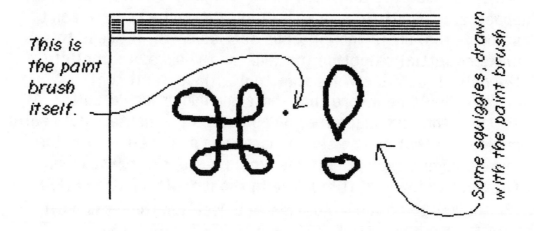

This is the paint brush itself.

Some squiggles, drawn with the paint brush

Try experimenting with the paint brush. Don't worry about how "good" your drawing looks for the moment. The important thing at this point is to just get used to the feel of the mouse as a drawing tool.

Once you have gotten comfortable with that, the mouse and the paint brush, you can erase the screen by double-clicking the icon that looks like this: ▱

Brush Patterns

One of the nicest things about the paint brush is that you can paint using any of the thirty eight different patterns at the bottom of the screen. To select a pattern, just point the arrow at the pattern you want and that pattern will appear in the larger box at the left end of the pattern boxes. The pattern that is in that box is the selected pattern and when you use the paint brush the brush will apply that pattern wherever you paint.

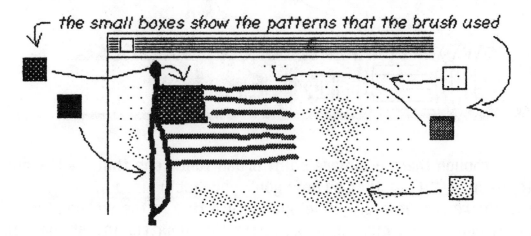

the small boxes show the patterns that the brush used

By changing the patterns the brush is painting with, you can create some very "colorful" drawings.

Painting Straight Lines

In addition to painting free-form lines with the paint brush as we have been doing, it is also possible to paint straight lines in any of four directions: up, down, left and right.

5

To make the paint brush paint straight lines, press the SHIFT key on the keyboard before you press and hold the mouse button. This will paint perfectly straight lines in any of four directions.

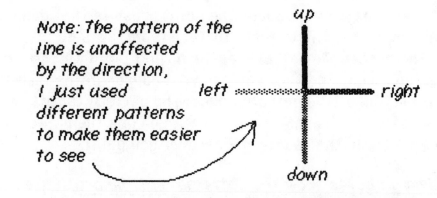

Note: The pattern of the line is unaffected by the direction, I just used different patterns to make them easier to see

up

left right

down

The Eraser

Although there are more paint brush functions that we'll want to discuss, I'll bet that by now you're probably tired of erasing the entire screen every time you paint a line in the wrong place. So, if you haven't already looked back into your Macintosh manual, here is a quick description of how to use the eraser somewhat more subtly.

First you'll need to click the eraser icon just once. This will darken the eraser icon, enabling that function. NOTE: In case you're unsure of which icon we're discussing, the eraser icon looks like this: ◿ . It's the same one you double-clicked to erase the entire screen.

Once the eraser is enabled, you will see a tool that looks like a small box on the screen. You can move the box to any location on the screen without erasing anything as you position it. When you press the mouse button, the dots that are under the small square will be erased. If you hold the button down and "drag" the eraser around on the screen, it will erase any dots that it passes over.

the eraser

erasing a path

Later we'll go over some other methods of erasing sections of your pictures that are even more refined than the eraser, but for now let's get back to the paint brush.

Different 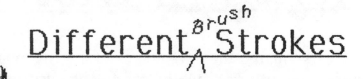 Strokes

Brush

No decent artist would ever consider putting a toolbox together with only one brush. So too, does MacPaint contain more sizes and shapes of brushes. To take a look the different brush shapes and sizes, a you need to do is double-click the brush icon. This will open the Brush Shape control window.

7

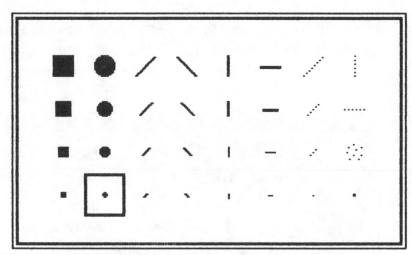

Brush Shape Control Window

As you can see, there are thirty two different brush shapes available for the paint brush. The one that is currently selected has a small box around it. To select another brush shape just click on it (point the arrow at it and press the mouse button). Let's experiment with some of the shapes...

Dots.....

By positioning the dots and clicking the mouse once, without moving, you will get single dots in the current pattern (whatever you have selected).

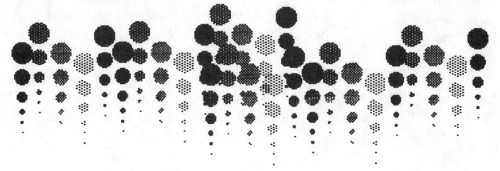

8

By overlapping black and white dots, you can produce small circles, crescents, moons, apple cores, etc.

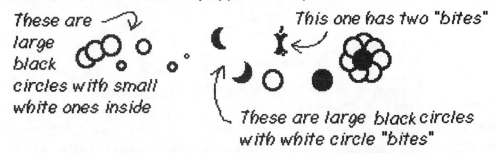

These are large black circles with small white ones inside

This one has two "bites"

These are large black circles with white circle "bites"

If you hold the mouse button down while you move the mouse, you will get smooth, continuous lines in any direction.

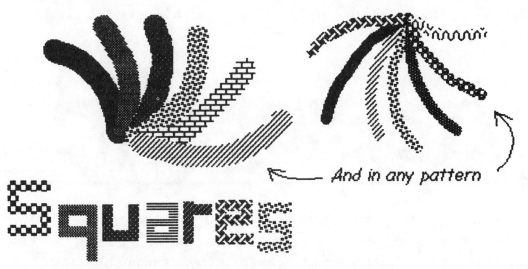

And in any pattern

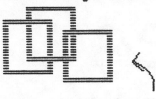

Square brushes can be used to create shapes that have corners and sharp edges. They work especially well with the SHIFT key (which makes straight lines).

These are straight (SHIFTED) lines

Small, overlapping squares in different patterns

9

Because squares are longer across the center than they are along their sides, diagonal lines will be thicker than vertical or horizontal lines drawn with square brushes.

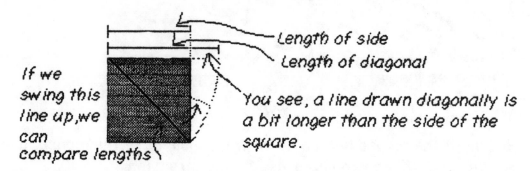

Length of side

Length of diagonal

If we swing this line up, we can compare lengths

You see, a line drawn diagonally is a bit longer than the side of the square.

Because of the difference in line widths, the square can produce lettering that has a hand-painted appearance.

Apples 5¢

As you can see, the squares can produce lines that are similar to the kind of crude brush strokes that would be made by a wide paint brush. For finer work, however, you will probably find that the diagonal line brushes are more like pen quills. These brush shapes can produce calligraphy-like lettering.

Diagonal Lines

If you look at the brush shape control window (back on page 8)

10

you'll find that there are four kinds of pen shapes. Two of them are diagonal and two are not (one is horizontal and the other is vertical). These correspond to holding a calligraphy pen in one of four positions.

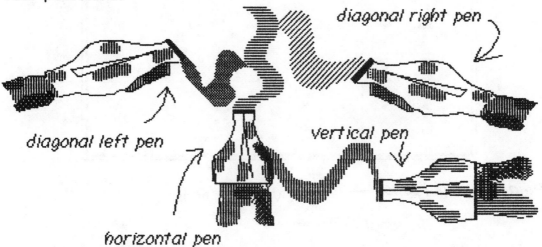

diagonal right pen

diagonal left pen

vertical pen

horizontal pen

By selecting different pen angles and pen sizes you can produce almost any of the standard calligraphic characters.

Big or small

By the way, if calligraphy isn't your cup of tea, you can also use these brushes to draw pictures such as:

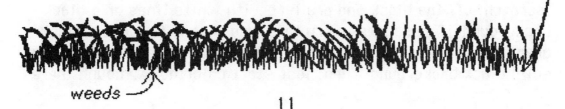

weeds

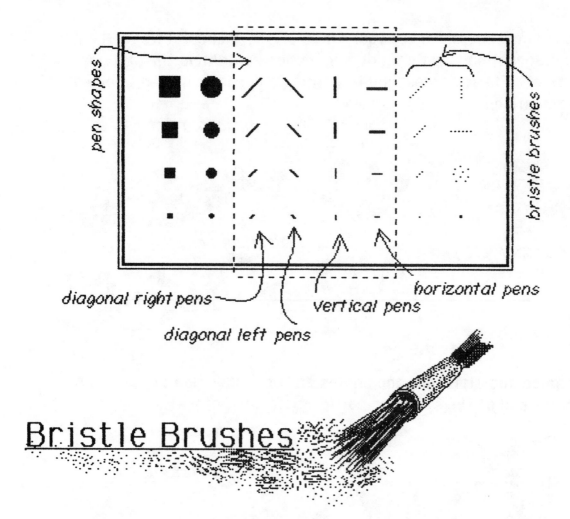

pen shapes

diagonal right pens

diagonal left pens

vertical pens

horizontal pens

bristle brushes

Bristle Brushes

The last brush types left to discuss are the bristle brushes (my term—not Apple's). These brush shapes produce either dotted brush strokes (if you click them on and off as you brush) or multiple lines (or scratches). These brush shapes remind me the most of scratch board. With scratch board, I usually begin with a black surface that has white underneath. To draw, you simply "scratch" off the black and are left with white lines on a black background. If you'd like to try this, you'll need to make a black area first. To do this, just get a large brush shape and select the solid black background. Then, just start coloring. Although there are several different ways to darken an area, for the sake of simplicity, just use the Paint Brush.

Hint: For these edges, use the SHIFT key so you'll get straight lines

Another thing that you can do with the bristle brushes is draw frames. The straight horizontal, vertical, and diagonal dotted lines produce parallel lines that really lend themselves to decorative borders.

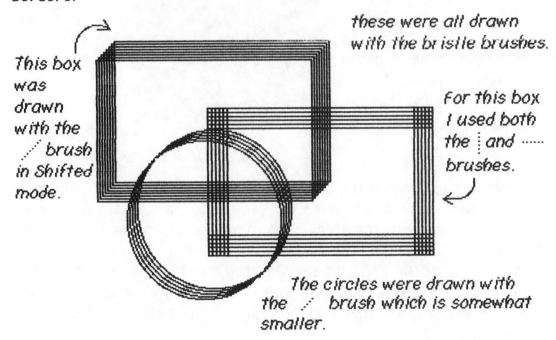

This box was drawn with the ⁄ brush in Shifted mode.

these were all drawn with the bristle brushes.

For this box I used both the ┊ and ⋯⋯ brushes.

The circles were drawn with the ⁄ brush which is somewhat smaller.

13

MacPencil Drawing

The Toolbox

Take a look at the MacPaint Toolbox. Directly to the right of the Paint Brush is a tool called the Pencil. The Pencil works a bit like the Paint Brush that's shaped like a small point. The biggest difference between the Pencil and the Paint Brush is that the Paint Brush always puts the selected pattern on the screen while the Pencil draws just one color at a time: black on white or white on black—and in just one size.

This icon represents the pencil

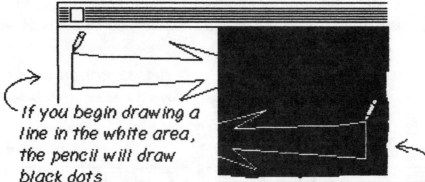

If you begin drawing a line in the white area, the pencil will draw black dots

But if you start in the black area, it will draw white dots

Notice that when the pencil was drawing black dots, the lines didn't show up in the black area. Similarly , the white dots that the pencil drew in the black area disappeared in the white area. If you are drawing a picture that runs from a black area to a white one (or vice versa) simply stop moving the mouse when you reach the border between the two areas and release the mouse. When you press the mouse button again, the pencil will draw in the right color.

14

LINES

The Line icon

Take another look at the Tool Box. Directly below the Paint Brush is a tool that looks like a diagonal line. That symbol is the icon for lines. MacPaint can draw lines any length (up to the size of a page) and any angle. Click on the line icon and it will darken. Now when you move the arrow into the work area, it will look like cross hairs. The center of the cross hairs indicate the starting point of your line.

To draw a line, start by putting the cross-hairs at one end of the line.

Then press the mouse button and hold it while you "stretch" the line to the exact location you want.

NOTE: Take a close look at the lines above. The ones that are at odd angles (most of them) are ever so slightly ragged in places. This is because the dots cannot be perfectly aligned in these angles. There are, however eight directions that will produce lines that are absolutely clean: Up, Down, Left, Right, and the angles that are precisely in the middle of these angles.

To get a better idea of why some lines look ragged and others look clean, here's an enlarged view of some lines:

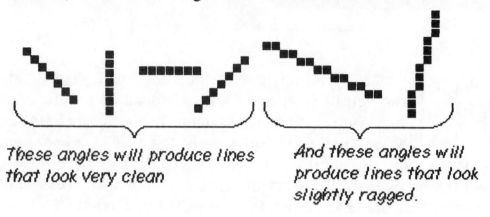

These angles will produce lines that look very clean

And these angles will produce lines that look slightly ragged.

To check this out, just hold this book out at arms length and squint your eyes.

To draw lines that fall into one of the eight "clean" angles just press the SHIFT key on the keyboard (as you did for straight painted lines) and "stretch" out your line. Notice that instead of moving smoothly as you change angles, the lines will "pop" into each of the angles as you approach them.

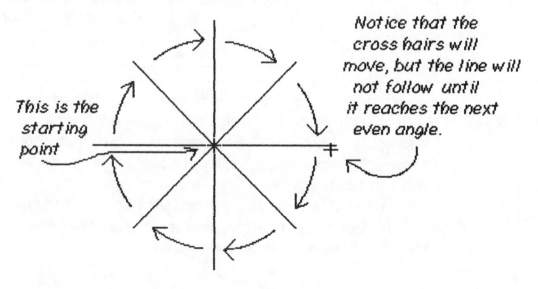

This is the starting point

Notice that the cross hairs will move, but the line will not follow until it reaches the next even angle.

16

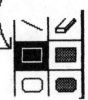

The Box icon

Right under the Line icon in the Toolbox, MacPaint has an icon that looks like a small rectangle. This is the Box icon. With it, you can make boxes in any size or shape that will fit in the MacPaint work area.

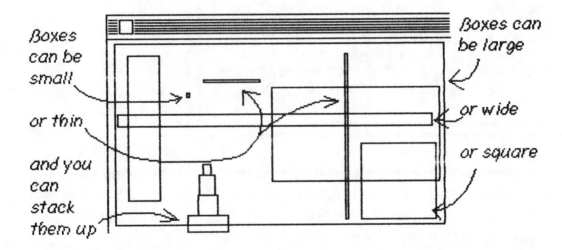

Boxes can be small

or thin

and you can stack them up

Boxes can be large

or wide

or square

To draw a square, click the Box icon. Then move the arrow into the work area (the arrow will become cross hairs, just as it did when you were drawing lines). Position the cross hairs so they mark the corner of the box you want to draw. Then press the mouse button and pull the box out until it is the size and shape you want. NOTE: You can pull the box out in any direction. For example, if you pull it up and to the right, the first corner will become the lower left corner of the box.

17

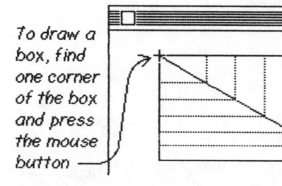

To draw a box, find one corner of the box and press the mouse button

Then, keep holding the mouse and drag the cross hairs to form the box you want.

Once you have gotten used to making boxes, click on the Rounded Rectangles icon(directly below the Box icon) in the tool box. This works pretty much the same way as the Box tool, but the boxes it makes have rounded corners.

These can be used in many ways, but rather than give you a lot of silly examples, I'll just let you experiment with them yourself.

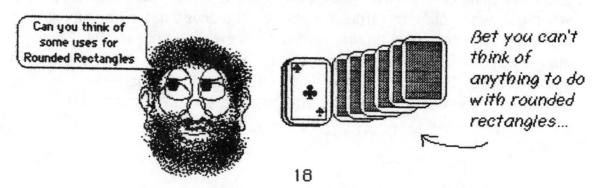

Can you think of some uses for Rounded Rectangles

Bet you can't think of anything to do with rounded rectangles...

Circles And other ROUND Shapes

Okay, now that we've explored all of the square-ish shapes, it's time we gave some attention to circles. Actually, MacPaint not only draws circles, it can draw almost any round shape from an oval to a circle.

As you can see, ovals can range from very flat to very round

Or they can be very tall and thin all the way to very wide and round...

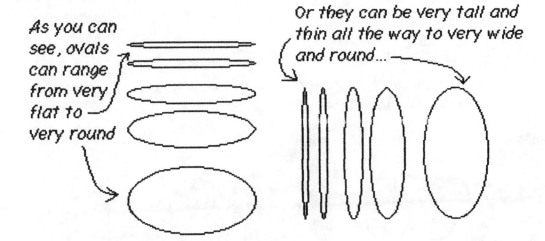

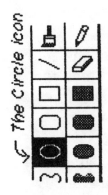

The Circle icon

To make a circle (or an oval) point the arrow at the Circle icon (just underneath the Rounded Rectangle icon) and move it into the work area. Once again, you will be using cross hairs.

The difference is that instead of the cross hairs locating an actual point on the circle, the starting point slides down as the circle (or oval) is formed. You then "pull" the circle out from the beginning point. As you do, the cross hairs locate a point on the "pulled" edge of the circle.

19

The further you "pull" the circle, the more the cross hairs "drift" away from the edge of the circle. What's actually happening is this:

The cross hairs define an invisible rectangle and the circle that is formed fits that invisible rectangle precisely.

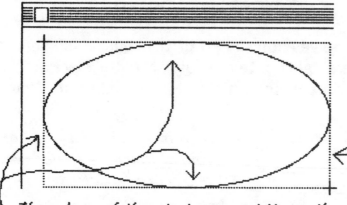

When you draw a circle with the circle tool, the cross hairs define an invisible rectangle

The edges of the circle or oval lie on the sides of the invisible rectangle.

↓ The Free-form icon

At first glance, you might think that the free-form shape tool is just about the same as the paint brush. You can draw lines in many different widths; the lines can be drawn in any direction and the shapes that it draws can be either open or closed.

It's true, these two tools are very similar, but there are subtle differences and it is the subtle differences that we'll look at here.

Subtle Difference #1: The Free-Form cursor is a cross hair while the Paint Brush can be any of thirty two different shapes.

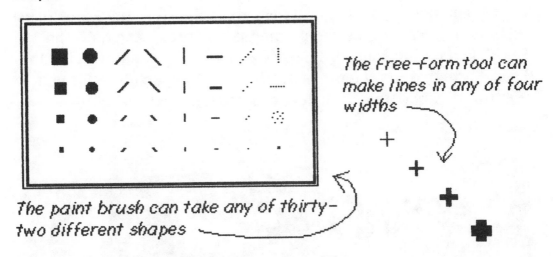

The Free-Form tool can make lines in any of four widths ⌐

The paint brush can take any of thirty-two different shapes ⌐

Subtle Difference #2: The Free-Form normally draws lines in black while the Paint Brush normally draws using the currently selected pattern.

Actually though, you can get the free-form tool to draw in the selected pattern by pressing the [Option] key on the keyboard. The trick is to press the option key first. Then put the cross hairs wherever you want to start drawing. From that point on, continue pressing the mouse button as you draw.

21

<u>**Subtle Difference #3**</u>: The third and final subtle difference between the Paint Brush and the Free-Form tool is the way they handle straight lines.

As you may recall from the previous section, the Paint Brush will paint perfectly straight lines if you press and hold the SHIFT key on the keyboard before and while you paint. With the Free-Form tool, on the other hand...sorry, no such luck, if you want a straight line: practice, practice, practice.

The connected line icon

Take a look at the heading above. The letters that make it up were drawn using the Connected Line tool. If you have ever tried to make a drawing using the Line tool and had trouble getting the lines to meet, this tool is for you.

The Connected Line tool is very similar to the Line tool but the next line you draw will always begin at the exact point the last one ended.

Okay, so how do you stop making connected lines if this tool always starts another line whenever you end one? (I hear you asking).

There are two ways to stop a series of these lines. The first

22

way to stop the connected lines is to connect with the starting point of the shape you're drawing. NOTE: This is a lot easier to do if you are drawing with thick lines.

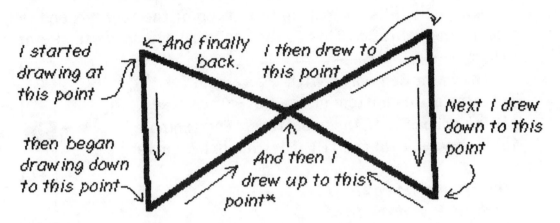

I started drawing at this point

then began drawing down to this point

And finally back.

And then I drew up to this point*

I then drew to this point

Next I drew down to this point

* If you try this, you'll find that the connected lines do *not* disconnect at the center of the figure where the lines touch. The line *must* connect to its starting point.

The other way of disconnecting connected lines is to move the tool right off the work area and into the tool box. Then all you need to do is click on any of the icons. NOTE: This will not "grab" the new tool, it will only disconnect the lines.

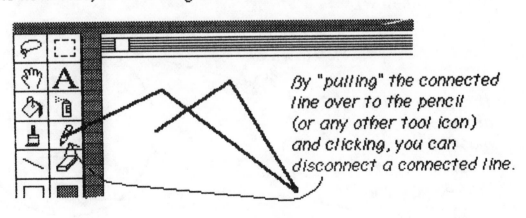

By "pulling" the connected line over to the pencil (or any other tool icon) and clicking, you can disconnect a connected line.

23

Paint Can

Okay, now let's go back up to the top of the tool box and take a look at the Paint Can. This is the tool directly above the Paint Brush.

The Paint Can works with the various patterns at the bottom of the MacPaint screen, filling shapes with those patterns. For example, let's draw an oval and fill it with a brick pattern.

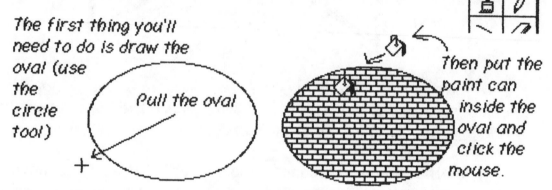

The first thing you'll need to do is draw the oval (use the circle tool)

Pull the oval

Then put the paint can inside the oval and click the mouse.

NOTE: The way that MacPaint knows where to paint is by the location of the tip of the paint coming out of the paint can (see the detail below).

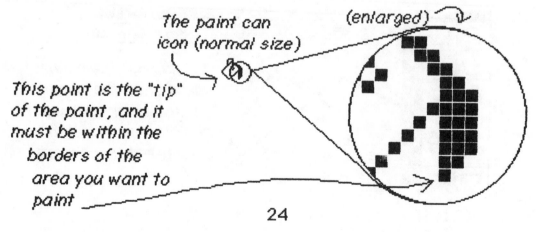

The paint can icon (normal size)

(enlarged)

This point is the "tip" of the paint, and it must be within the borders of the area you want to paint

A Word On: Patterns

On the last page, we filled an oval with a brick pattern (one of the patterns at the bottom of the MacPaint screen). The trouble is, I haven't really explained how to select these patterns. So if you don't already know, here is the method.

The selected pattern shows up here

There are thirty eight different patterns available in this palette of patterns

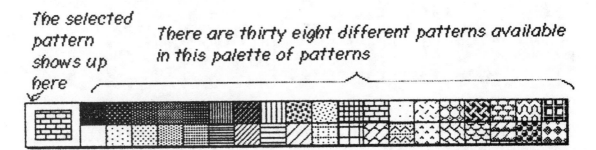

To select one of the patterns, point the arrow at the pattern you want and click the mouse button once (not twice—we'll cover what double clicking these icons does in the next section). Once you select one of the pattern icons, that pattern will appear in the large box at the left end of all of the patterns.

Incidentally, this works with the paint brush and any of the other tools that can use the patterns.

Back to the Paint Can ➡

In addition to painting the inside of shapes, the paint can is able to paint the lines themselves as long as all of the dots that you want to paint are made up of connected dots. NOTE: The dots in the line(s) must be connected side to side, dots that are connected diagonally will not be painted.

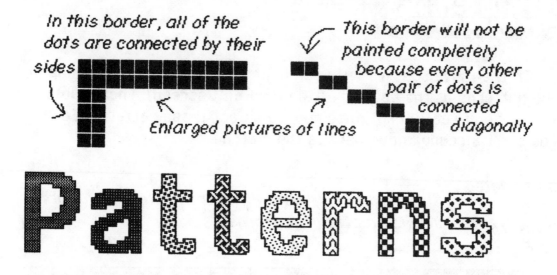

In this border, all of the dots are connected by their sides

This border will not be painted completely because every other pair of dots is connected diagonally

Enlarged pictures of lines

Patterns

Well, as I promised, here is the section on using the patterns. Before we start into all of the finer details of patterns, let's take a moment to look at those tools that can use the patterns, and how they use them.

1) PAINT CAN:

The paint can always fills shapes with the selected pattern. You don't have to do anything special, just put the paint can into the area you want painted (or on a line that you want painted) and click the mouse button.

2) SPRAY CAN:

We haven't discussed the use of the spray can yet, however, it uses the patterns in a very special way and we'll cover that later. For now, don't worry about it.

3) PAINT BRUSH:

Like the paint can, the paint brush will always use the selected pattern.

4) LINES:

Although lines are normally drawn in black, they can be drawn in any of the selected patterns by first pressing the OPTION key on the keyboard.

5) HOLLOW SHAPES: (□, ⬭, ◯, ♡ and ◁)

These are the five lower, left-hand tools in the tool box. Like lines, these normally draw black lines, but will use the selected pattern if you press the OPTION key before you start drawing.

6) FILLED SHAPES: (▣, ⬬, ⬤, ♥ and ◀)

These are the five lower, right-hand tools in the tool box. In operation they behave just like the hollow shapes except, after you have finished drawing your shape, it is filled with the currently selected pattern.

Custom Patterns

Look at the letters in the heading "Custom Patterns" above. If you take a really close look you will see that each of the letters is filled with a different pattern. Now look at the patterns along the bottom of the MacPaint screen. None of the patterns used in these letters can be found among the standard MacPaint patterns.

The patterns that were used in making the "Custom Patterns" heading are all custom patterns. Although the patterns are easy to create, there are a few rules that you'll need to know about.

27

First, while thirty eight patterns may seem like a lot, for every new pattern you create, you'll lose one old one.

Second, although the patterns can be used to fill very large areas, each is made up of a single design that fits into an 8 × 8 grid (64 dots).

Last, the patterns that you produce will be saved with the MacPaint document when you save it, but will not appear on other documents unless you make them from a copy of the original... if this last point seems confusing, don't worry, just read on, it'll become clearer as we continue.

Saving Old Patterns

Okay, even though this section is all about creating and saving new patterns, there is a possibility that you'll want to use some of the old patterns that came with MacPaint at some future time. So, assuming that you will want to use the old patterns again, begin by opening a MacPaint document and, (for the sake of simplicity) we'll call the file: Old Patterns. To do this from the desk top, double click on the MacPaint icon, and when the page called Untitled appears, pull down the File menu until the words "Save As" are highlighted. Then let go of the mouse.

This is the File menu from the list of menus at the top of the MacPaint screen. Although the File menu is not specifically a MacPaint topic, we'll be using it a lot, and as such, we'll cover it throughout the book.

button and you'll get the following message:

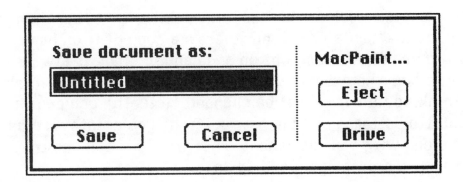

Don't worry about the fact that MacPaint named your file "Untitled", also, DON'T press RETURN or click any of the buttons—just type in the name you want to give the file (Old Patterns). After you've typed in the name, either press RETURN or click on the button that says SAVE. These both have the same function and MacPaint will only let you do one or the other.

When the Save As window disappears, you will find that the MacPaint document you are working on is now called "Old Patterns". This also saved a document called "Untitled." Ordinarily you will probably use the SAVE function to save a file that you produce with MacPaint. However, if you have changed a file and want to save both the new and the old copy, you can use the Save As function. This will leave the original unchanged and will create a new file for the new picture.

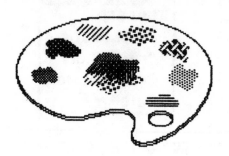

The MacPaint Palette

Take another look at the MacPaint palette that runs along the bottom of the MacPaint screen (there's a copy of it on page 25 if you don't have MacPaint up and handy). Since it always seems to come up exactly the same way, it's easy to be misled into thinking that it cannot be changed. Actually, you can change the palette patterns and the new patterns you create will be saved along with your document. That way, you can use the patterns you create again and again

New Patterns

Okay, now that you're interested, let's make some new patterns so we'll have something to save in our new MacPaint file.

30

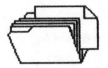 # Opening MacPaint Files

To begin this session, we'll need to open the file we made earlier called "Untitled." Depending upon what you're doing, there are at least two ways to open a file. Since we haven't gone into this in detail before, let's take a moment to look at how this is done.

If you are on the desk top (first screen that comes up when you turn on the Macintosh—it has icons for the disk you entered and perhaps some of the files in that disk) you can open a MacPaint file in one of four ways.

1) To Open a New MacPaint File:

Point the arrow at the MacPaint icon and click the mouse button once. Then point the arrow at the menu at the top of the screen labeled Files. Pull down the arrow until the word Open is highlighted (actually, darkened). Then let go of the mouse button and MacPaint will OPEN a new file called "Untitled."

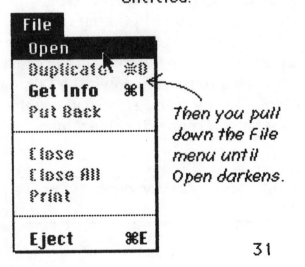

Then you pull down the File menu until Open darkens.

First you click once on the MacPaint icon

2) Opening an Existing MacPaint File:

Point the arrow at the file that you want to OPEN and click the mouse button once. Then (as you did before), point the arrow at the File menu, press the mouse button and pull down the menu until the word Open is highlighted. When you let go of the button, MacPaint will be loaded in from the disk and the MacPaint file that you selected will appear in the work window.

File	
Open	
Duplicate	⌘D
Get Info	⌘I
Put Back	
Close	
Close All	
Print	
Eject	⌘E

Then you pull down the File menu until Open darkens.

To Open an existing file, point the arrow at the icon for that file

Untitled

3) Opening a New File the Quick Way

To Open a file more quickly (using fewer steps) point the arrow at the MacPaint icon and double-click the mouse button. This process is an alternative to pulling down the File menu so don't look for the menu after you double-click, the whole screen will clear, menus and all.

To Open a file without pulling down the File menu, just double-click its icon.

MacPaint

By the way, this works for almost any file or utility.

4) Opening an Existing File the Quick Way

Double-click the icon for the MacPaint file you want to Open

Interestingly, the method for Opening an existing file is identical to the method for Opening a new file-with one small difference. Notice that when you Opened a new file, you double-clicked the MacPaint icon. To Open an existing file, just double-click that icon instead of the MacPaint icon.

To keep things as simple as possible, if you are at the desk top right now, double-click the icon called "Untitled". If you are still in MacPaint, stay put - there are several methods of Opening files from within MacPaint also and you might just as well learn them now.

1) To Open a New File From MacPaint

To exit a file, just point the arrow at this small box and click the mouse button

If you are currently in a file and you want to Open a new one, you will first need to exit that file. Of course, there are a couple of ways to do this. You can either, click the small box in the upper left-hand corner of the work area...

or you can point the arrow at the MacPaint File menu (don't confuse this menu from the File menu on the desk top) and pull down to

the word "Close". If you have not already saved the
file, MacPaint will ask you if you want to save the
file with this message box.

When you
get this message
box, it's usually
best to click the
box marked "Save"

Otherwise you
stand a chance of
losing the file.

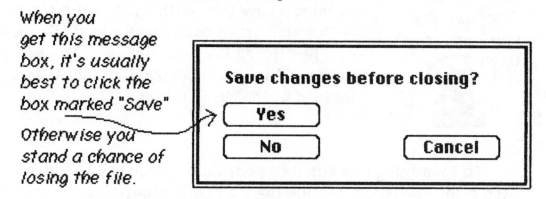

Save changes before closing?

Yes

No   Cancel

In general, it's a good idea to save files when you
leave them. That way you'll be sure to have a copy
of the file containing all of your most recent
changes. The only times you would not want to
save a file are : 1) If you won't have any more use
for the file and you want to get rid of it; 2) If you
made a major mistake and you don't want to save
it; or 3) You have a copy of the file and you didn't
make any changes this time (perhaps you just
printed the file).

So, depending on what you want to do, click in
the appropriate box (Cancel returns you to the
same file).

Once you have saved (or not saved) the file, the MacPaint work
window should disappear. If it doesn't, you made a mistake—go
back and try again. If the window did disappear, point the arrow
at the File menu again and this time, pull down to the word Open.
This will Open an existing file. Note: If you want to Open a new
file, pull down to the word New instead...simple, right? ... RIGHT!

Whenever you see menu options that are gray, it means that you cannot select them at that time.

Note: This File menu is not the same as the Macintosh File menu (see desk top on page 32).

Now, to Open a file, pull down this menu until the word Open is highlighted. When you let go of the mouse button you'll get the File Selection window:

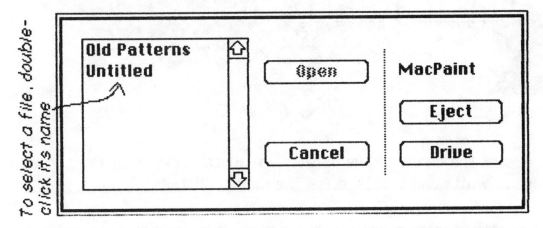

To Open a file that is listed in this window, just point the arrow at its name and double click the mouse button. That name will be highlighted and then the window will disappear. A few moments later, the picture will appear in the work window.

NOTE: MacPaint pictures actually fill an 8½"x 11" page, however, the work area is only a portion of that. To see the whole page, either double-click the Grabber (the hand-shaped icon in the tool box) or use it to re-position the screen—more on this later on.

All right, just one more comment and then we'll get on to the pattern-making. If you look back at page 35, you'll see that there is a button called "OPEN." That button is gray at first, but if you single-click a file name it will become black (on a white background)—in other words, you could click that option. This is an alternative to double-clicking a file name to Open it.

Making Patterns

Point the arrow at the palette box at the bottom of the screen that is white and double-click the mouse button.

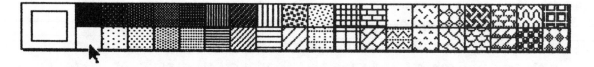

This will do two things: first, it will select that pattern and make it the current pattern (any tools that use a pattern will use that one) and second, it will put a control window in the middle of the MacPaint screen. This is the window that lets you change the patterns. There are two boxes in this window, one that says OK under it and another that says Cancel. Since we chose the white (empty) pattern, these boxes will both be white. In fact, the left-

36

hand box shows an enlarged view of the pattern and the right-hand box shows the actual pattern, repeated throughout. Although you cannot see it, the left-hand box is divided up into a grid, 8 dots high by 8 dots wide. Pointing the arrow and clicking the mouse button at these dots will make them switch colors (from black to white and back again).

Note: The dotted lines that you see in this illustration are here to help you see the relative positions of the dots. They do not appear in the window on the screen.

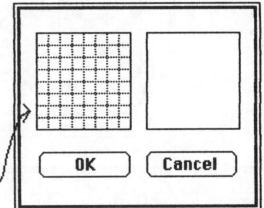

Now, let's practice making a pattern. Point the arrow some-where inside the left-hand box in the window and click the mouse button once and release it immediately. A small, black square should appear in that location in the left-hand box and an array of much smaller black dots should appear in the right-hand box. If you point the arrow anywhere else on the screen and press the mouse button, (except in the OK or Cancel boxes) the computer will "beep".

Keep on putting dots in the left-hand box until you get a pattern that pleases you in the right-hand box.

To erase a dot, release the mouse button and then point at the

37

dot you want to erase. Now click the mouse button and the dot will turn white. Whenever you click a dot, it switches colors. If you click and hold the mouse button, the arrow will continue painting in the color that was initially selected until you let go of the button and click it again.

By entering a pattern on this side with the arrow

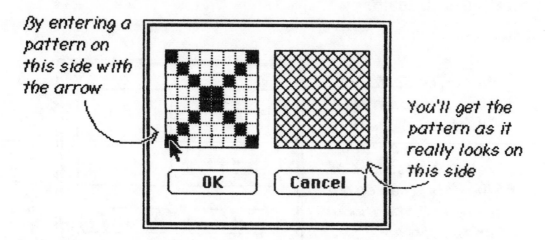

You'll get the pattern as it really looks on this side

Once you have a pattern that you want to use, save it by clicking the OK button (directly below the left-hand box). Now look at the palette of patterns at the bottom of the screen, your new pattern has replaced the original plain, white pattern.

Copying Patterns

Two more things that you should know before you go off copying and disposing of patterns is how to copy existing patterns and which ones you'd be better off keeping—and why.

First of all, there are nine patterns that are more than just patterns. They can be used to produce a grey scale. Although we

38

haven't used them yet, we will very soon. Grey scales are used for shading pictures. The shading heps to give them a 3-dimensional appearance.

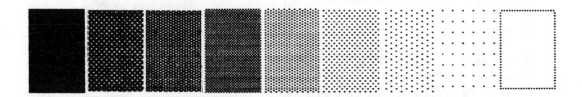

If you keep these nine patterns, you'll still have room to make 28 patterns of your own.

As it turns out, MacPaint has only got room for 38 patterns at a time in the palette, however, you can save patterns like chips of paint on a document. Then, when you want to use one of the patterns, all you need to do is copy it.

To copy a pattern, first, select a pattern from the palette (this is the one we'll be replacing) by double-clicking its box. Now use the arrow and point to any place on the screen that is inside the work area but outside the control box.

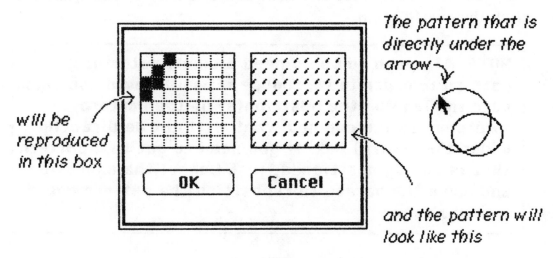

will be reproduced in this box

OK   Cancel

The pattern that is directly under the arrow

and the pattern will look like this

To get a better idea of how this works, make a series of boxes along the right side of the screen and fill each of them with a different pattern.

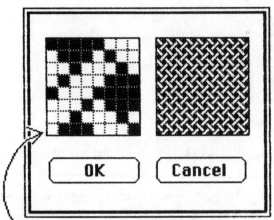

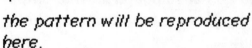

the pattern will be reproduced here.

So by following this process, you can produce an entire page of MacPaint patterns to be used at any time. All you need to do to put them into your palette is select (double-click) the pattern that you want to replace and then point to the one you want and click the mouse again.

NOTE: Although you only need a small patch of a pattern in order to reproduce it, you should use some care in planning the position(s) of the pattern swatches so the one you want will not be directly under the control box. If you need to get to a pattern that is poorly positioned, just Cancel the operation and move the screen to reposition the pattern you want to copy.

A Potpourri of MacPatterns

This page is more for fun than anything else. The boxes you see here are the enlarged images that you'd see in the left-hand box of the pattern control window. Try entering some of them, you may be surprised by the way they look when they are reduced.

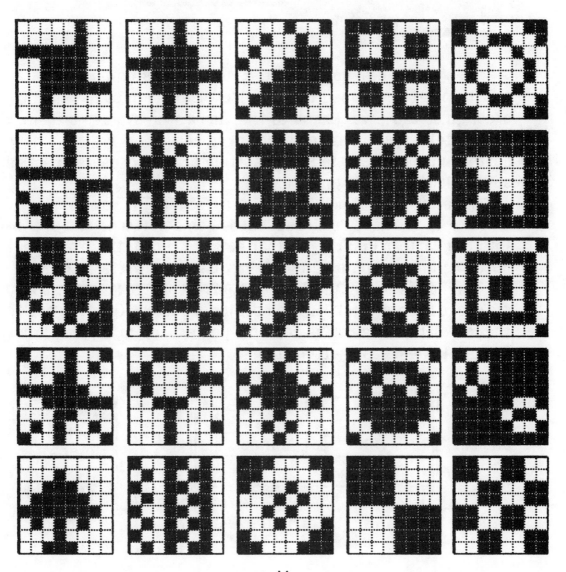

Saving the Palette

Now, once we've gone to the trouble of designing new patterns for the palette, we may want to use them again some time. In order to do that, we'll need to find some way of saving them. Well fortunately, that's already been taken care of. If we put a new pattern into the palette at the bottom of the screen, it will be saved along with the picture.

To get an idea of how this works, let's try it now.

Note: if you haven't already made some patterns and put them into the Pattern Palette, do that now. To recap, the way to put patterns into the palette is to first choose a pattern that you don't mind losing (actually you've got a copy of it in the backup disk) and double-click it. Then design a pattern (or copy one from the last page. Once you've copied a pattern, point at the OK button and click the mouse button again.

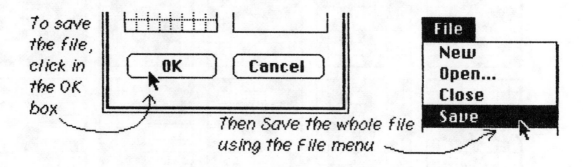

To save the file, click in the OK box

Then Save the whole file using the File menu

| File |
| New |
| Open... |
| Close |
| Save |

NOTE: After you initialize the Save function (from the **File** menu) MacPaint will ask you to name the file; call this file **Pattern Master.**

Once you have Saved the file, pull down the File menu until the word Quit is highlighted. This will exit MacPaint and return you to the desk top.

Now you'll need to find the pattern that we just saved. If you don't see it's icon, it may still be hidden in one of the folders on the desk top, or it may simply be out of view in one of the windows.

In case you are unsure of how to track down elusive files, let's go over the process now.

To begin with, here's a slightly reduced picture of the desk top with all of the files "put away" (not currently displayed).

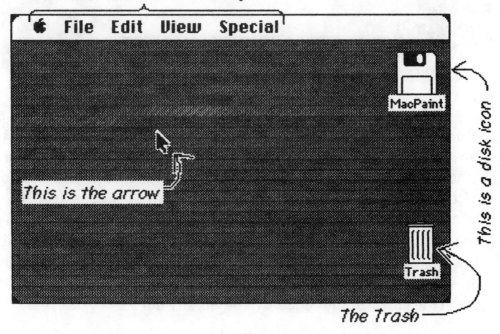

These are the menu headings

This is the arrow

This is a disk icon

The Trash

Along the top of the screen (in the white area) you'll find four menu headings and a flashing apple symbol (⌘). In the grey field below the headings you'll find icons for the disks that have been logged into the Macintosh (inserted and read); the trash can icon (which is used to delete files) and the arrow icon (which is akin to but not quite the same as the cursor on some other computers).

To take a look at the files that are on the disk, point the arrow at the disk icon and double-click the mouse button).

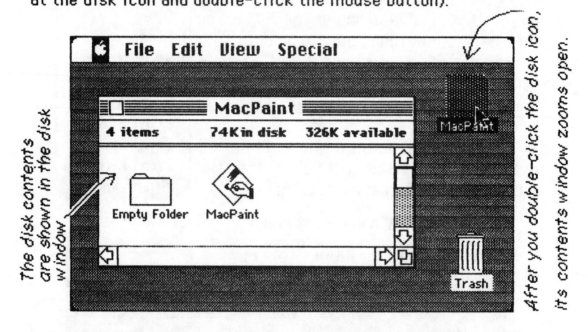

The disk contents are shown in the disk window

After you double-click the disk icon, its contents window zooms open.

Take a close look at the disk window above. It has four arrows along its edges; one in the upper right-hand corner; one in the lower left-hand corner and two in the lower right-hand corner. When one of the scroll bars (along the right edge and the bottom of the window) is grey (instead of white) it means that there are more files in the window than can be viewed at one time. To see the hidden files you can either enlarge the window by pointing at the size box (⊡) in the lower right-hand corner of the window or by scrolling the window up (⬆) or down (⬇) with one of the scroll arrows at the ends of the scroll bars.

Note: The left (◁) and right (▷) scroll arrows won't work in the screen on the last page because the scroll bar between them is white.

Looking through the
Files

In addition to "hiding" in the windows, MacPaint documents can be tucked away in one of the various file folders that may be on the desk top. The folder icons look like the icon on the last page that was called "Empty Folder". To open a file, point the arrow at it and double-click the mouse button. The files that are in the folder will appear in that folder's window. Try this now with the Empty Folder.

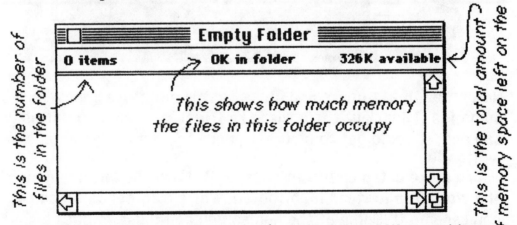

The Empty folder (by definition) contains no files and has therefore got no icons, but other folders would contain file icons.

show the number of items in the folder, how much memory they use and how much memory is left on the disk.

So far it looks as though the folders do nothing other than make it hard to find documents. Well, in a sense that's true since they won't be just laying on top of the desk top in plain view. On the other hand, the Macintosh desk top can get just as messy as any other desk and if you don't find some way of organizing your files it won't be long before your desk top looks like this:

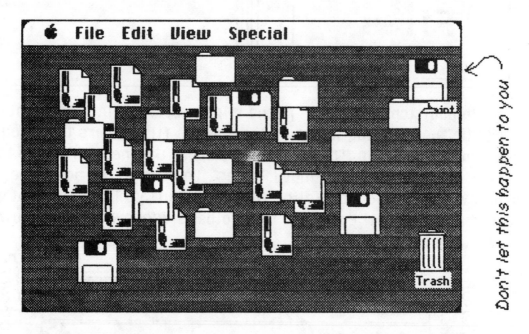

Don't let this happen to you

Now, the files, folders and disks that are pictured above are all dummies (I just put them there to illustrate a point) but as you can see, it could get to be pretty hard to find things after a while.

To make extra empty folders, pull down the **File** menu until the word **Duplicate** is highlighted. While a folder is black you can rename it. Some of the names you could use might be programs to store MacPaint, MacWrite or whatever programs might be on your disk.

46

To put a file or document into a folder, point at the file and press the mouse button. Then, while you are holding the mouse button down, drag the icon over to the folder until the folder becomes black, then let go of the mouse button.

By the way, you can use the duplicate function to make extra copies of anything on the desk top except disks and the trash. If you do make a copy of a document Mac will name it "Copy of..." whatever the name of the original disk was. You can then rename it if you like.

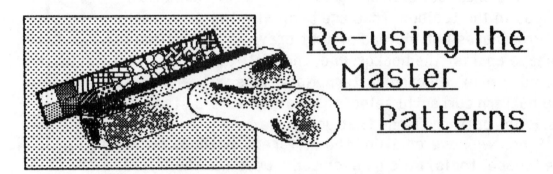

Re-using the Master Patterns

Now, after you have organized your desk, let's take another look at the file that we made earlier called Pattern Master. It has all of the new patterns that we'll want to use in future MacPaint documents. Any copies of Pattern Master will have the same palette it has when they are opened. So to re-use the patterns in Pattern Master, use the **Duplicate** function from the **File** menu. Open the files by double-clicking them instead of MacPaint. Of course, if you want to use the standard MacPaint patterns, double-click MacPaint.

Pattern Mas
Copy of Pattern Master

To use your special patterns, make a copy of Pattern Master and double-click it.

MacPaint

otherwise, just Open (double-click) MacPaint.

FILLED Shapes

Filled shapes are directly to the right of the hollow shapes in the toolbox. They are basically the same as the hollow shapes but instead of just drawing the outline of a shape against the background, they fill that shape with the currently selected pattern. Note: This will work with any pattern currently selected whether it is a standard MacPaint pattern or one that you made.

Since we covered all of the different methods of using the "shape" tools, let's go over some uses for the filled shapes instead of re-hashing techniques you already know. Note: If you don't quite remember how to use some of these, re-read pages 17 thru 23.

These are the filled shapes

Over-lapping Shapes

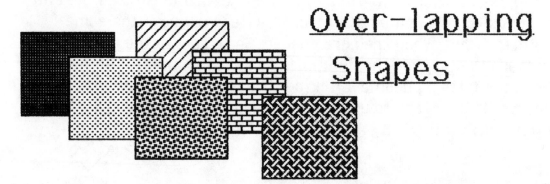

Probably the most interesting thing about using over-lapping shapes is the three-dimensional appearance it gives to your drawings. To produce these, first draw a filled shape (like one of the boxes in the heading for this section. Depending on the affect you want, you can use different line widths for the shapes and either emphasize the edges of the shapes...

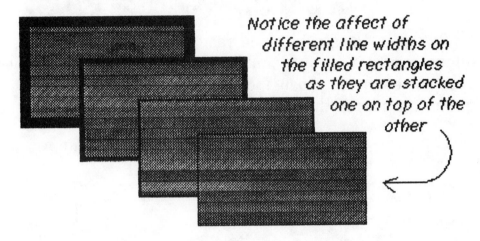

Notice the affect of different line widths on the filled rectangles as they are stacked one on top of the other

or eliminate the edges altogether.

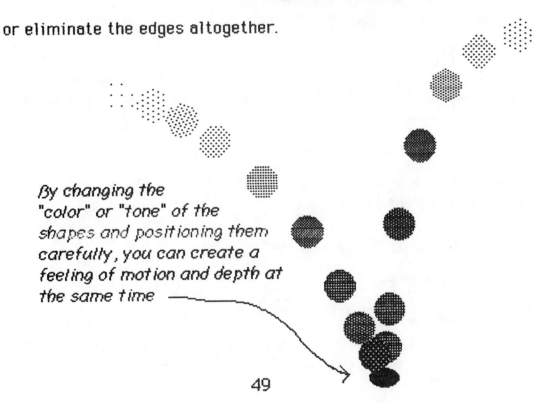

By changing the "color" or "tone" of the shapes and positioning them carefully, you can create a feeling of motion and depth at the same time

49

Adding Thickness

On the last page, we made shapes that produced a three – dimensional affect by placing one shape in front of another. A second method for producing three – dimensional drawings is by giving the shapes thickness. This makes them appear to "stand out" from the page.

Let's begin by drawing a cube from two filled, white squares.

First, select the plain, white pattern and then, using the filled box tool (▧) draw two white squares, one in front of the other.

Notice that the hollow square tool will not give the over-lapping affect (☐).

Now, using the line tool (＼), connect the upper two and lower left corner of the two squares.

Be careful to align the corners

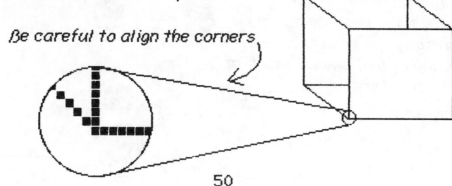

50

Now remove the two lines that "cut through" the sides of the cube by carefully using the eraser tool (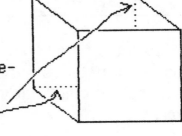).

The lines that need to be erased are shown dotted in the picture above.

Notice also that most objects are lighter on top than they are on the sides.

To finish up the picture of the cube, we can add some shading to its sides to help give it some depth. Note: Generally speaking, darker shades appear to recede (drop farther back) and lighter shades move forward.

Although there are some real similarities between the regular, filled and hollow shapes (circles, ovals, squares and rectangles), the irregular, filled shapes are very different from their hollow counterparts. While the outlines the two kinds of tools produce are the same, there are some peculiarities in the way that they become filled.

Fortunately, MacPaint uses some consistant rules regarding what part of the shape gets filled and what part doesn't, so it will be easy to demonstrate them with just two examples.

Example #1:

Both the filled free-form tool and the filled connected line tool work in two steps. First you draw the shape, then, after it is complete, MacPaint will fill it. Let's take a look at how this works...

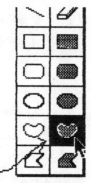

This is the filled, free-form tool

To begin with, you'll need to select the filled, free-form tool. Then move the arrow into the work area (the tool should become a cross-hair). After you've made sure that you have the tool properly selected, move the pointer down to the supplementary tool box in the lower left-hand corner of the MacPaint screen. This is the line-width selection box (we used it to select different line width with the line tool earlier).

Notice the check mark in the box. This indicates the selected line width. The width we want to select is the single-line width (the second one down - it's the one selected in the picture). To change line widths, point the arrow at the line width and click the mouse button once.

Select the single-line width

Okay, we're almost ready to begin drawing a filled free-form shape. Just one more thing first - select a pattern other than black or white from the palette (black and white don't work quite as well as one of the other patterns for this example). Now move the pointer back into the work area and try to draw a shape that is similar to the one below. Notice how none of the lines cross themselves. Make sure none of yours do either. You'll see why in a moment.

Notice that MacPaint waited until you were done drawing before it filed your shape.

52

Now select the filled, connected line tool from the tool box. It works very much like the hollow, connected line tool, but like the filled free-form, after you've finished drawing the shape, it'll be filled with the currently selected pattern.

After you've selected the connected line tool, go ahead and make a shape like the one below (as before, make sure you don't cross any of your lines).

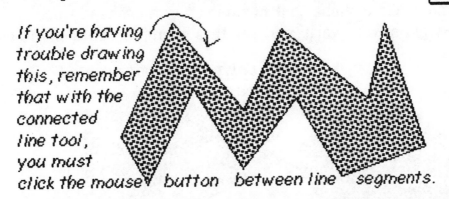

If you're having trouble drawing this, remember that with the connected line tool, you must click the mouse button between line segments.

This is the filled, connected line tool

Once again, notice that the shape wasn't filled until you finished drawing it. By the way, if you had some trouble getting this tool to end, remember that it won't stop drawing until you either connect the line with its starting point or pull the line out of the work area and into the tool box (and click the mouse button).

Before we go on to the next example, let's review what we just covered.

First, with free-form shapes, you simply select the tool, put the pointer (cross-hair) into the work area and start drawing. Don't forget to select a pattern and line width first.

On the other hand, although the connected line tool is set up the same way as the free-form tool, you must click the mouse button each time you want to end a line segment.

Finally, in both of the cases above, we didn't cross any of the lines we drew.

Example #2:

In the example on the last page, I told you NOT to cross any of your lines. The reason that I told you that was because MacPaint treats areas that are formed by crossed lines differently from the unbroken areas.

So you see what I mean, select the free-form tool again and this time, make a shape that has one or two crossed lines. Figure-eight's work very well for this example... this one is on its side.

At this point, MacPaint created two shapes

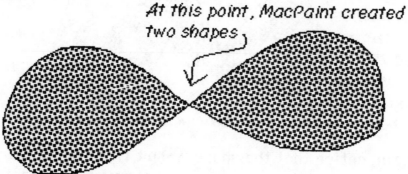

Notice how crossing your own line created two separate areas in the example above. If you try some more complex shapes, you'll find that each time you cross a line in your drawing, you create another separate area that will be filled by MacPaint.

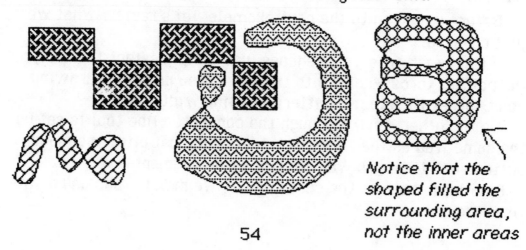

Notice that the shaped filled the surrounding area, not the inner areas

Interesting Feature:

One thing that you may or may not have noticed while you were experimenting with the filled shapes is that while the connected line tool requires you to precisely finish each shape at the exact point it began, the free-form shape will actually finish the shape for you if you don't close the shape. Try this:

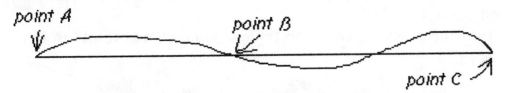

point A   point B

point C

I drew the wavy line from point A (above-left) to point B (above-right) and then let go of the mouse button. As soon as I released the mouse button, MacPaint drew line C (the straight line) connecting the ends of my drawing and creating the three areas. The reason the shape is empty is because I selected the white pattern for this example to emphasize the lines. By the way, this technique works just as well with the hollow free-form tool.

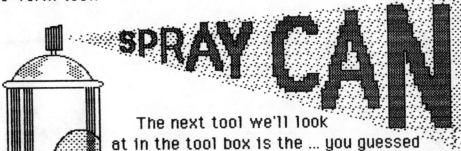

SPRAY CAN

The next tool we'll look at in the tool box is the ... you guessed it - spray can. The icon for the spray can is located directly above the pencil icon and just to the right of the paint can.

Like the paint can and the paint brush, the primary mode of spray can operation uses the currently selected pattern from the palette. Incidentely, the spray can can also use any custom patterns that you may design.

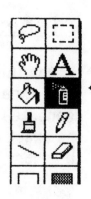

The spray can

For an idea of how the spray can works, point the arrow at the spray can icon and click the mouse button. When you move the arrow into the work area it will become a small patch of random dots resembling a spray pattern ( ).

Select the black pattern and try spraying some "paint" in the work area.

These darkened spots were made using repeated circular spraying

Notice how spraying in one spot longer than others cause that spot to darken up.

Now try selecting different patterns from the palette and spraying with them.

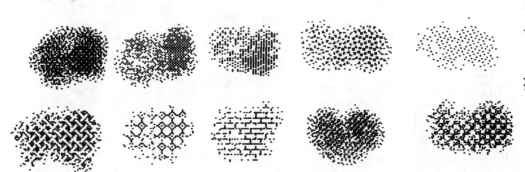

In each case (above) spraying for a longer time in one spot brought out the pattern that was being used. By spraying first in one pattern and then in another, you can actually "blend" patterns together.

56

Take a look at the heading above. The shading behind the
lettering was created by mixing shadings (from dark to light)
with the spray can. To get a feel for how this works, try using
the flat gray shade (fourth from the left in the top row of the
palette) with the lighter gray right below it.

*This shading was done by
just* spraying *one pattern
over the other. Notice how
the second pattern covers
first one.*

*This shading was done
using the ⌘ key on
the keyboard (just to
the right of the Option
key.*

If you look closely at the two shading examples above, you'll
see that the right-hand spot is made from the same two patterns
as the left-hand spot, but the middle of the right-hand spot has
a pattern that was produced adding the two shades to each other.
Pressing the ⌘ key on the keyboard has the effect of painting
over an existing drawing rather than obscuring it.

As you try mixing different patterns, notice how each
new, resulting pattern is generally a bit darker than either of the
original patterns.

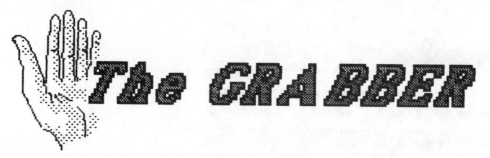

The GRABBER

Just above the paint can, on the left-hand side of the tool box is a funny-looking icon that resembles a hand. Apple calls this icon the grabber. The reason they call it the grabber is because that's exactly what it does...it grabs the picture.

Why (you might ask yourself) would one want to "grab" the picture?

The answer is simple: To move it around. In other words, the grabber "grabs" the picture and lets you drag it around, pulling the picture right out of view if you like.

Grabber pulls the picture away from the edge of the work area.When you let go of the mouse

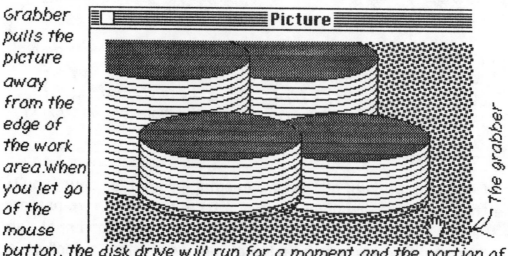

Picture

The grabber

button, the disk drive will run for a moment and the portion of the picture that was out of view will be filled in.

Up to this point, we've been limited to drawing in a relatively small work area. By using the grabber, we can move the work area around on the screen and draw anywhere on the page.

58

Grabbing Small Objects:
the Lasso and the Selection Box

In addition to the grabber, MacPaint has two other tools that are designed to let you move smaller sections of your pictures around within the work area. These tools are called the lasso and the selection box.

The selection box works a lot like the rectangle (square) tool. To use the selection box point at its icon and click the mouse button. Like the rectangle tool the selection box uses a cross hair. To use it, move the cross hair to one corner of the area that you want to select and press the mouse button. Hold the button down while you pull the selection box open to surround the area you want to select.

The selection box

Watch the selection box. Once the area has been selected, the box will stop flashing

After you have selected the area that you want to "grab" and move, let go of the mouse button and move the pointer to a place inside the selected area. When the pointer changes from a cross hair to an arrow, press the mouse button and the arrow will "grab" the marked area.

59

Look at the picture on the previous page. Notice that the selection box "grabbed" all of the dots in the area that it selected.

The lasso, on the other hand, only grabs the dots that are black. In other words, it only grabs the picture, not all of the dots around it. To get a better idea of the difference between the selection box and the lasso, take a look at these pictures:

When you "select" an area with the selection box, you get the whole area, including the white parts. As a result, the blank area can cover other areas.

On the other hand, when you use the lasso, only the actual picture will be selected and as a result, only the picture will cover up anything under it.

60

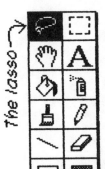

The lasso →

In addition to grabbing just the picture itself, the lasso can also grab an area of almost any shape even if it is very close to some irregular objects. This is something the selection box can't do since it always "grabs" areas with straight sides.

Take a look at the example below. In the upper picture, we're trying to "grab" a bird. Unfortunately, it is so close to the tree that we cannot grab the bird without grabbing a chunk of the tree with it.

In this drawing, the selection box got the bird, tree and background.

using the lasso to "pull down just the bird.

In this case, all we "grabbed" was the bird because we could carefully trace its edges and then move without affecting any of the background.

61

This is the font icon

The last tool in the tool box is the font. Actually, the font (my term, not Apple's) represents lots of fonts (type styles) that can be used to type in MacPaint. The font icon looks like a large letter A and is just above the spray can and to the right of the grabber.

Actually, we won't be covering all of the features of the MacPaint character set(s) in this chapter. For more information on how they work, see Chapter Four: Font.

For now, though, let's at least get used to typing messages with MacPaint. First, point the arrow at the letter A in the tool box and click the mouse button. Then move the arrow to the work area and it should turn into an I-beam.

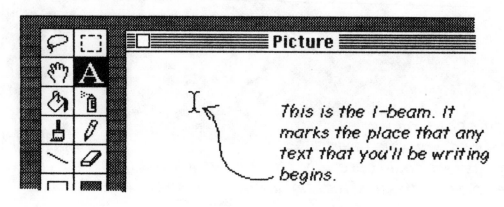

This is the I-beam. It marks the place that any text that you'll be writing begins.

Put the I-beam in the location that you want to begin writing and click the mouse button. This will put (what Apple calls) an insertion point on the screen.

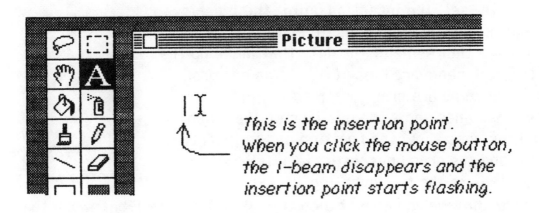

This is the insertion point. When you click the mouse button, the I-beam disappears and the insertion point starts flashing.

One thing that can be very difficult, is positioning text in exactly the right place. This is because the text aligns with the insertion point and the insertion point aligns with the I-beam but none of them are ever on the screen at the same time...whew!

So, in an effort to make the relationship between these various objects clear, take a look at the drawing below.

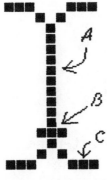

The parts of the I-beam

A: *The vertical bar of the I-beam marks the left margin of the text you will be entering. Each time you press the RETURN key when you are entering text, you will return to a point one line down and directly below this line.*

B: *This horizontal bar marks the bottom of your text. All of the letters' bottoms will align with this.*

C: *The lowest bar marks the location for descenders (ie. the tail of a lower-case "j").*

Now let's look at the insertion point. You'll never see these together on the screen (as they are here) because once you click the mouse button to "set" the insertion point, the I-beam disappears. If you look closely at this drawing, you'll see that some of the dots that make up the enlarged I-beam are black (■), some are gray (✳) and some are gray, trimmed in black (▣). The black ones show the position of the I-beam, the gray ones show the position of the insertion point and the gray ones with black trim show points where the two over-lap.

Position of the insertion point relative to the I-beam

Now that we've had a chance to look at how the I-beam and the insertion point line up, let's take a look at how the letters fit in. First, MacPaint has many different letter sizes and styles. As a result, the I-beam cannot possible specify the exact position of each entire letter. This is partly because different size letters require more or less space and also each different letter in each of the character sets take up more or less space.

Notice that the "W" is quite a bit wider than the "I"

and the "t" is quite a bit taller than the "u"

So as a result, the I-beam only designates the lower-left-hand corner of the first character that will be typed. Note: In fact, since different characters are different shapes and sizes, the first character will not always fit right into the corner made by the I-beam.

64

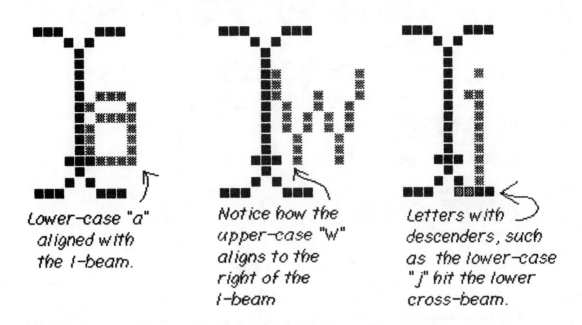

Lower-case "a"
aligned with
the I-beam.

Notice how the
upper-case "W"
aligns to the
right of the
I-beam

Letters with
descenders, such
as the lower-case
"j" hit the lower
cross-beam.

Okay, that's all for the tool box. In the next chapter we'll be covering the **Edit** menu (at the top of the MacPaint screen). In much the same way that a word processor gives you the power to manipulate words, the **Edit** menu of MacPaint lets you manipulate pictures.

If you went through this chapter and felt that you wanted more on the tool box... Good! This chapter was just a short introduction on how the tools work. In Chapter Seven: Techniques you'll learn much more about what you can do with the tools. For now, however, on to **Edit**.

CHAPTER

TWO

Chapter Two: The Edit Menu

At the top of the MacPaint screen, you'll find seven menu headings, an Apple, File, Edit, Goodies, Font, FontSize, and Style. Each of these with the exception of the Apple and File has a chapter of its own. The reason the Apple and File are not covered in separate chapters is that the Apple is not specifically a MacPaint topic and File is covered in one way or another in most of the chapters. To learn more about Edit, read on...

OK

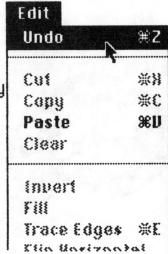

Imagine that you've just spent two or maybe three hours drawing a picture with MacPaint and all of a sudden (perhaps because you're getting tired) you draw a line that just about obscures the center of your drawing. Time to give up...right?

Wrong!

Hidden in the deep recesses of your Macintosh, MacPaint has saved a copy of your picture. If you do something...in fact almost anything and for some reason, you don't like it—point the mouse button at the **Edit** menu (near the upper left-hand corner of the and pull down the menu until the word Undo is highlighted. This will swap your picture with the hidden copy...without the error.

Look at the Edit menu (on the right). Some of the menu items are written in black and the others are written in gray. When a menu selection is gray, you can't select it. Fortunately, menu items will only be gray when it makes absolutely no sense to select them anyway.

Incidentally, you may have noticed that over to the right of the word **Undo** there's a (⌘) symbol and the letter "Z." As a matter of fact, several of the menu items have that symbol and a letter beside them. By pressing the (⌘) and the letter indicated (at the same time) you can get the menu item without pulling down the menu.

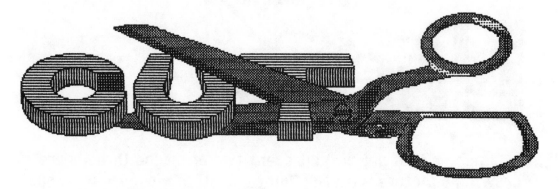

The next item down in the Edit menu is Cut. Cut allows you to select a section of a picture and remove it. You can select an area to be cut using either the Selection Box or the Lasso.

This section was "Cut" using the lasso. Notice that the area that was removed is irregular. The lasso can cut any area that you can outline by hand.

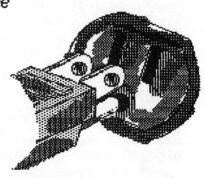

On the other hand, the area that was cut with the Selection Box is perfectly rectangular.

68

Just so you're absolutely sure how to "Cut" an area out of a picture, let's practice cutting right now. First, we'll need a picture to "Cut" from. Since this isn't an exam and what the picture looks like doesn't really matter, draw something simple for this example...like the filled rectangles we used in Chapter One.

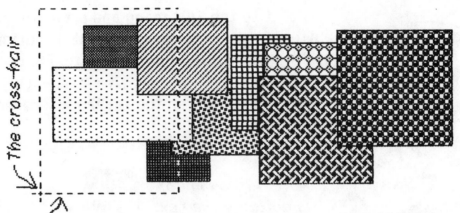

The cross-hair

(For this example, use the Selection Box to select an area

Once you've selected the area to be "Cut", pull down the menu until the word "Cut" is highlighted. Note: You could have alternatively pressed ⌘ and the X key on the keyboard.

After you let go of the mouse button, disk drive will whirr for a moment and the area you selected will disappear. The reason that the disk drive runs for a few seconds is that it is saving the section you "Cut" in a temporary file. That way, if you want to put the section somewhere else, it will be in memory and you can just put it there – more on this later.

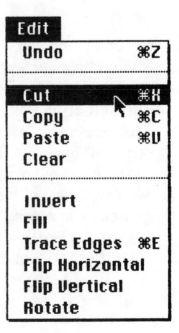

Edit	
Undo	⌘Z
Cut	⌘X
Copy	⌘C
Paste	⌘U
Clear	
Invert	
Fill	
Trace Edges	⌘E
Flip Horizontal	
Flip Vertical	
Rotate	

PASTE

Point to the Edit menu and press the mouse button. If you look down the list of options you'll find a heading called Paste. Paste takes section of a picture that was recently "Cut" and puts it back on the screen wherever you want.

Note: Although Copy is actually the next option in the Edit menu, we're skipping to Paste because it will be easier to understand Copy once we've covered Paste.

Edit	
Undo	⌘Z
Cut	⌘H
Copy	⌘C
Paste	**⌘U**
Clear	
Invert	
Fill	
Trace Edges	⌘E
Flip Horizontal	
Flip Vertical	
Rotate	

One thing you should be aware of is that when you use the Selection Box to "cut" a section of a picture, it will be "pasted" back, white space and all. "Cut" the picture in Lasso mode and just the picture will be "pasted" MacPaint remembers how you cut something, you should think of where you will be putting the picuture later, not only how you will "Cut" it. Sometimes it is harder to "Lasso" something out of a picture, but impossible to fit it into its new location without the lasso.

70

To get a better idea of what I mean, let's "Cut" and "Paste" a few pictures and see how MacPaint handles each one. First, let's look at some filled rectangles again.

In this example, we want to remove the dark rectangle, put a smaller, lighter one in its place and put the dark one above the others.

Begin by select-ing the Selection Box. Put the cross-hairs in one corner of the rectangle

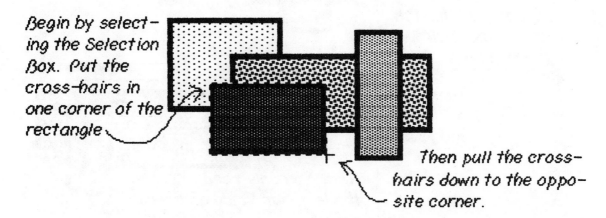

Then pull the cross-hairs down to the oppo-site corner.

Now, to remove the selected rectangle, either pull down the Edit menu until "Cut" is highlighed or press ⌘ and the letter "C" on the keyboard.

We'll need to re-draw the two rectan-gles that were partly "Cut" by the dark one.

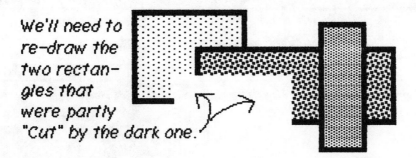

Before we can add the small rectangle, we'll need to "repair" the two rectangles that were behind the dark one. To do this, select the the pattern that matches one of the rectangles and re-draw it. Note: Since you'll be covering one rectangle with the other, it's best to begin with the one that is furthest back.

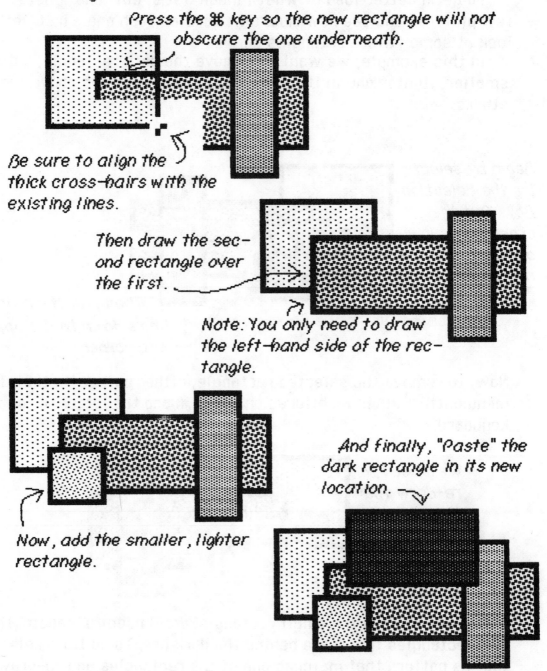

Press the ⌘ key so the new rectangle will not obscure the one underneath.

Be sure to align the thick cross-hairs with the existing lines.

Then draw the second rectangle over the first.

Note: You only need to draw the left-hand side of the rectangle.

Now, add the smaller, lighter rectangle.

And finally, "Paste" the dark rectangle in its new location.

In the previous example, we were able to "Cut" and then "Paste" the shape we wanted using the Selection Box since it was rectangular. But if the shape we want to move is irregular the Selection Box may not be able to "paste" it properly.

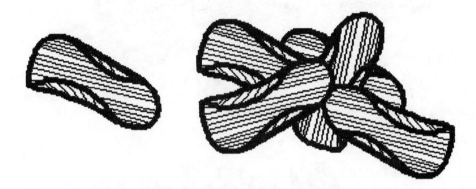

What we want to do is add the object on the left to the pile of objects on the right. Of course we could select the left-hand object using the Selection Box, but if we did, then we'd get a white rectangle on top of some of the objects in the pile.

As you can see, the white area that was selected along with the object was moved over onto the pile also.

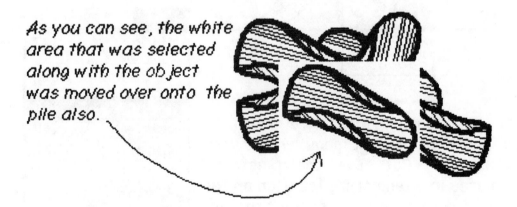

To avoid this, begin by selecting the object to moved with the lasso. Although it may be a bit more trouble, you will not be moving anything but the object itself.

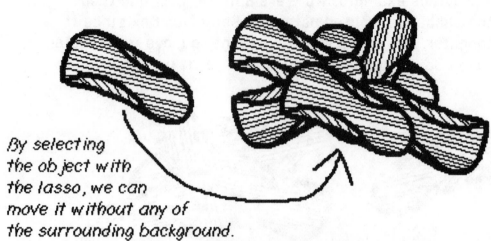

By selecting
the object with
the lasso, we can
move it without any of
the surrounding background.

Making Copies

The "Copy" option (which is directly
above "Paste" in the Edit menu) works very
much like "Cut". "Cut" saves the selected
picture area in a temporary location on the
disk and then deletes that section from the
screen.

Copy also saves a selected portion of

Edit	
Undo	⌘Z
Cut	⌘X
Copy	**⌘C**
Paste	⌘V
Clear	
Invert	
Fill	
Trace Edges	⌘E
Flip Horizontal	
Flip Vertical	
Rotate	

the picture in a special file in the disk. The difference is that "Copy" doesn't delete it from the screen.

This is especially useful if you want to put two copies of a drawing in two different places on a sheet of paper that are so far apart that you cannot get them both in the work area at the same time. Note: If you're copying a picture and it will wind up somewhere in the work area you don't need to use "Copy", you can simply select it and "drag" it over with the pointer as we did in Chapter One.

Edit	
Undo	⌘Z
Cut	⌘H
Copy	⌘C
Paste	⌘U
Clear	
Invert	
Fill	
Trace Edges	⌘E
Flip Horizontal	
Flip Vertical	
Rotate	

Notice that Cut, Copy, Paste and Clear are all grouped together. That's because they all do similar things. Clear (the only one that we haven't discussed) also acts on an area that can be selected by either the Selection Box or Lasso and its effect is very much like "Cut". The difference is that "Clear" doesn't save the area anywhere. Once its gone...it's gone.

The advantage of "Clear" is that if you "Cut" or "Copied" a picture earlier that image will not be changed.

75

Invert

Point the arrow at the Edit menu and press the mouse button. Now look at the six options at the bottom of the menu. These are grouped together because they are image editing commands. If this term is unfamiliar to you, it's not surprising...I just made it up. What I mean is that you can use these commands to modify the pictures that you draw with MacPaint.

The first of the six image-editing commands is Invert. Invert reverses the color of every dot in a selected area. Note: all six of the image-editing commands require either the Selection Box or the Lasso to select the area to be modified.

Edit	
Undo	⌘Z
Cut	⌘H
Copy	⌘C
Paste	⌘U
Clear	
Invert	
Fill	
Trace Edges	⌘E
Flip Horizontal	
Flip Vertical	
Rotate	

This is the image as it was drawn

This image was selected, using the Lasso. As you can see, only the actual image was reversed, but since part of the image was solid black, it disappeared into the white background.

This image was selected with the Selection Box, as a result, the backround was reversed along with the image.

76

The three examples on the previous page show a simple drawing and the way that Invert affects it depending upon how it was initially selected. If you look at the original drawing, the legs on the close side of the bumble bee are outlined while the ones on the far side are solid black. As a result, when the image was inverted using the lasso, the legs that were solid black disappeared...why?

Let's take a closer look at how invert works. The picture below is an enlarged view of a simple pattern.

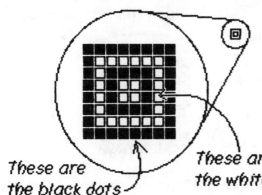

Now, when we invert this pattern, all of the dots (squares in the enlarged view) that are black will become white and all of the dots that are white (open squares in the enlarged view) will become black.

These are the black dots

These are the white dots

When you select an image with the Selection Box, it selects the dots inside it including the white background dots. Note: The Selection Box also selects the dots that lie under the flashing border.

This picture shows the image above after it has been selected by the Selection Box. All of the dots pictured are selected.

These are the dots between the Selection Box and the image we made

This is the image itself.

This is the Selection Box (enlarged).

77

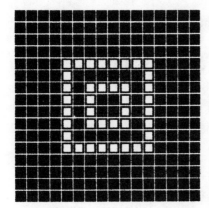

The picture on the left shows the results of inverting the selected image on the previous page. Notice that all of the dots within the selected area have been reversed.

Another thing that you should be aware of is that the outer row of dots in the original drawing (which had been black) became white after reversal.

Unlike the Selection Box, the Lasso selects just the image—not its background. Actually, that is not quite true. To be even more specific, the Lasso selects every black dot. All of the white dots remain untouched.

So when we select the shape with the lasso, all of the dots that were within the selected area are reversed.

Note: Any white dots that are completely enclosed by a black shape are also selected and will be reversed when the image is inverted.

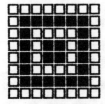

As you can see, all of the dots in the image are reversed. This results in the outer row of dots being white against a white background. In other words, they will not be visible and the final image will appear to be smaller than the original.

This is exactly the same thing that happened to the bumble bee a couple of pages ago. The legs that were white on the inside and black on the outside were still visible after reversal because the white parts turned black. However, the legs on the other side of the bee disappeared because they became white on white.

78

The fill command is right below the invert command. Once again, Fill behaves differently, depending on how the area to be filled is selected.

Since we began with the Selection Box last time, let's look at how Fill affects an area selected by the Lasso first.

Edit	
Undo	⌘Z
Cut	⌘H
Copy	⌘C
Paste	⌘V
Clear	
Invert	
Fill	
Trace Edges	⌘E
Flip Horizontal	
Flip Vertical	
Rotate	

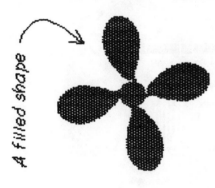

A filled shape

The shape on the left was drawn and then filled (using the paint can) with one of the patterns from the palette. Once all of the petals have been filled individually, there is no way (short of erasing all of the dots, one at a time) to fill it with a new pattern. To confirm this, get the pencil and draw a shape. Then fill it with the pattern you see in the picture above and then try to use the paint can to fill it with another pattern.

It won't work.

The reason that you can't re-fill an area is because the paint can looks for black dots and uses them as its boundries. Since a pattern is made up of lots of dots, most of them will stop any other pattern at the point it's entered.

79

Select the shape you drew on the last page with the lasso. Then select a pattern from the palette (other than the one we used earlier). Note: the shape you lasso'ed will still be selected. Now, point at the Edit menu and pull down until Fill is highlighted and then let go of the mouse button.

This will fill the shape with the new pattern.

Notice that the shape was filled inside and out with the selected pattern.

Over-Filling a Shape

Re-select the shape above (the one we just filled with the 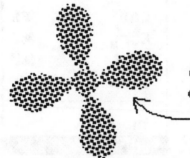 pattern.

Now select another pattern such as ■ and pull down the fill command from the Edit menu. As you can see, this does not look like the pattern we chose.

We got a broken-up pattern because of the way that lasso selects a shape...black dots only. So when we re-selected the shape and then re-filled it, the gray pattern was only painted into each of the small dots that made up the shape.

Fill-ing with the Selection Box

Draw a shape...any shape and select it with the Selection Box and select a pattern from the pattern palette. Now pull down the Edit menu until the word Fill is highlighted.

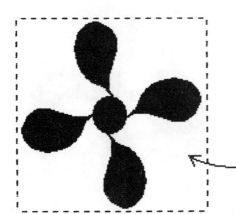

This is a shape that is similar to the one we used on the last two pages. Notice that it has been selected with the Selection Box

PRESTO!...When you let go of the mouse button, the entire area inside the Marquee is filled with the selected pattern. Clearly this option is different from Fill when we select a shape using the lasso. However, we can't use it for filling shapes.

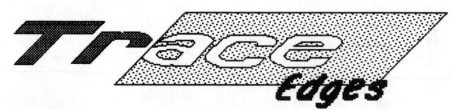

Edit	
Undo	⌘Z
Cut	⌘H
Copy	⌘C
Paste	⌘U
Clear	
Invert	
Fill	
Trace Edges	**⌘E**
Flip Horizontal	
Flip Vertical	
Rotate	

Draw another small sketch (you can use the one from the last page if you still have it) somewhere near the center of the MacPaint work area.

You don't need to use the same sketch as before, any drawing will do.

Now select that shape with the Selection Box.

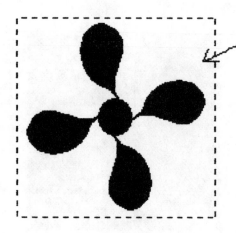

Note: For this function, you must use the Selection Box. The Lasso cannot perform this function.

Then pull down the Edit menu until the words Trace Edges are highlighted.

When you let go of the mouse button, you'll
find that the shape you had before has been
erased but its outline remains.

What happened is that MacPaint drew a
line around all the edges of the shape,
and then removed the shape itself.
Note: If you select a shape with the lasso and pull
the menu down to Trace Edges, you will find that
menu option is gray and cannot be used. Trace Edges
will only work with the Selection Box.

Now select the traced shaped with the Selection Box and re-
trace its edges.

This drawing was traced once

*If you trace the edges of a shape
more than once, the traced edges will
be traced over and over again
eventually resulting in a picture
that only remotely resembles the
original.*

This drawing was traced twice

*and this one was
retraced nine times*

FLIPPING
FLIPPING

FLIPPING

Edit	
Undo	⌘Z
Cut	⌘X
Copy	⌘C
Paste	⌘U
Clear	
Invert	
Fill	
Trace Edges	⌘E
Flip Horizontal	
Flip Vertical	
Rotate	

The Flip options

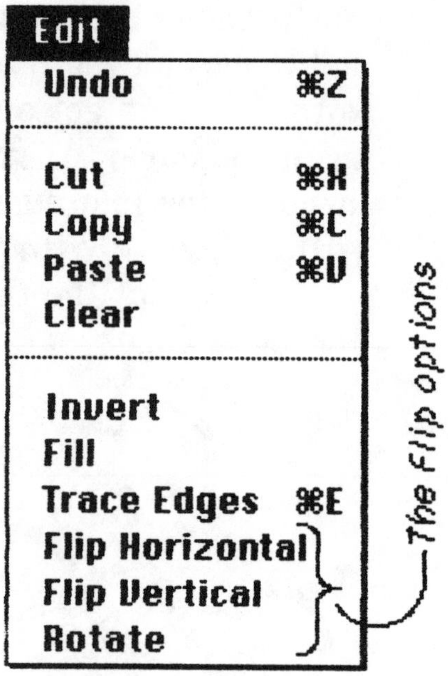

Take a look at the Edit menu (pictured at right). The last three options it lists are called:

Flip Horizontal
Flip Vertical
and
Rotate

Although each of these functions work slightly differently, they all have a similar effect—they change the position or the direction of a shape or shapes.

To begin with, let's look at Flip Horizontal. In order to use this function, you'll need to select a shape (draw one first if you haven't got one) with the Selection Box.

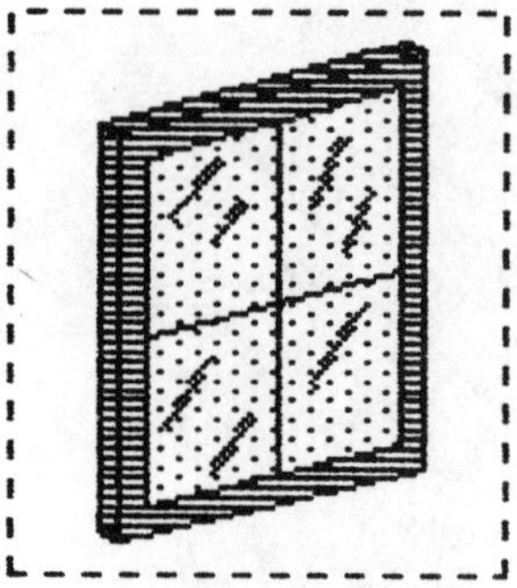

Note: You must use the Selection Box to select shapes. These three functions will not work on shapes that you select with the Lasso.

84

Pull down the Edit menu until the words Flip Horizontal are highlighted and then release the mouse button. The flip functions take the image you select and turn over end-for-end in the direction you specify.

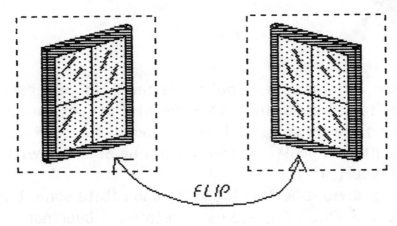

Flip Horizontal takes any image that is selected by the Selection Box and flips it over from right to left.

FLIP

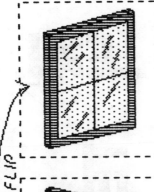

Select the first picture again. Now pull down the Edit menu again, but this time, pull down until the words Flip Vertical are hignlighted.

Flip Vertical takes any image that you select with the Selection Box and flips it over from top to bottom.

FLIP

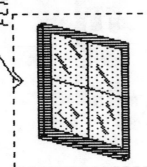

By using various combinations of Flip Vertical and Flip Horizontal, you can create mirror images of this picture in any of four different directions.

85

At first glance, it might seem that if we can "Flip" our images in any of four different directions, that "Rotate" is just another way of doing the same thing. In fact, that is not the case. Rotate gives us four additional positions that cannot be attained with either Flip Horizontal or Flip Vertical.

To see these positions better, let's flip and rotate some text instead of a picture. This will help us to retain our bearings.

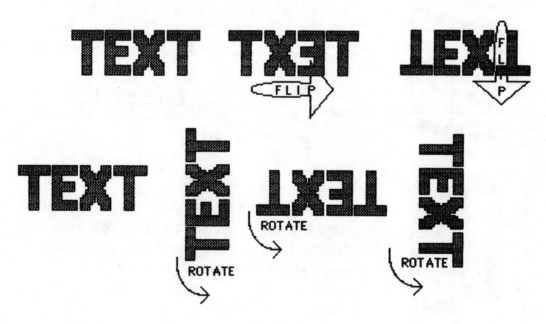

WORD	ꓒꓤOꟽ	MOᴚD
(WORD vertical)	(WORD ꓒꓤOꟽ vertical)	(ꓒꓤOꟽ vertical)
ꓒꓤOꟽ	(ꟽOᴚD WORD vertical)	OᴚOꟽ

The chart to the left shows all nine positions that you can produce using a single image. Notice that no two are exactly the same.

If you want to experiment with these yourself, begin by drawing or writing anything. Then make two copies of the original, flipping one of the copies horizontally and the other vertically. Then make three copies of each of the three images and rotate each of the images, first one rotation, (actually a quarter-turn) then two rotations and then three rotations.

This will give you eleven copies of the original, however three of the copies will be duplicates. See if you can determine which they are and why they came out the same.

CHAPTER THREE

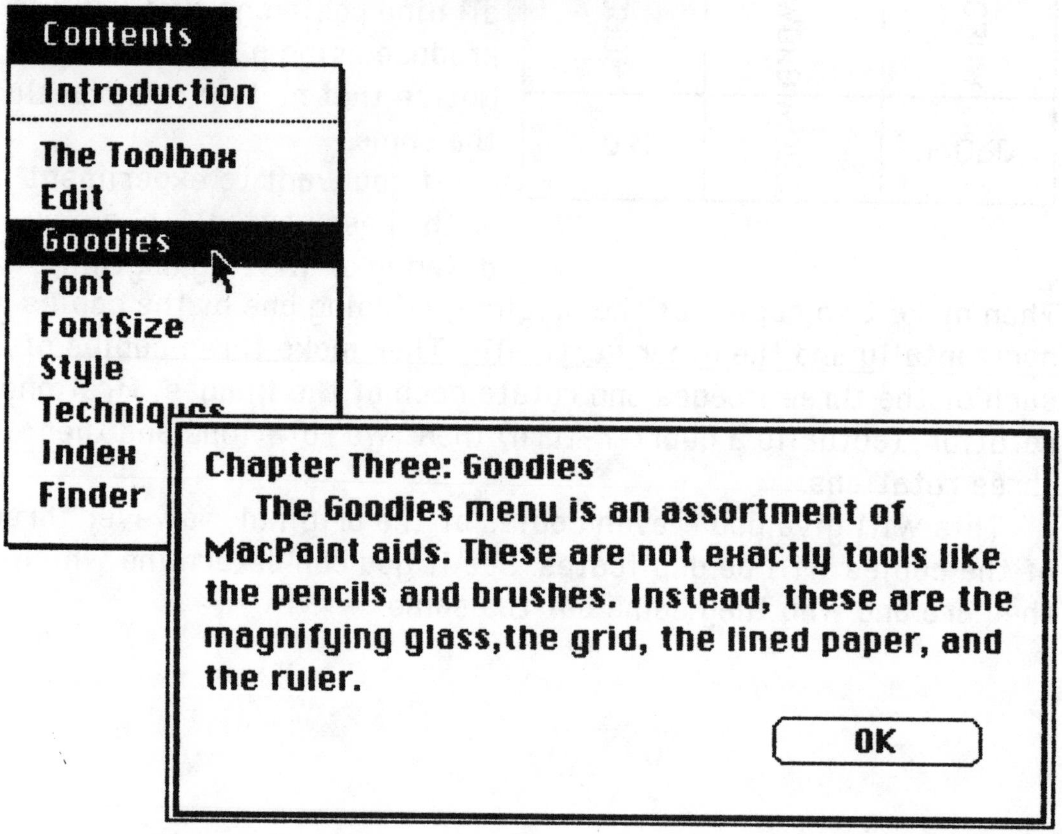

Contents
Introduction
The Toolbox
Edit
Goodies
Font
FontSize
Style
Techniques
Index
Finder
Chapter Three: Goodies
The Goodies menu is an assortment of MacPaint aids. These are not exactly tools like the pencils and brushes. Instead, these are the magnifying glass,the grid, the lined paper, and the ruler.
OK

Working our way from left to right, the next menu heading on the MacPaint screen is called Goodies. Goodies are (as I said on the chapter, title page) for the most part drawing and painting aids. However, even that description is not quite complete since some of the Goodies are tool-like. Perhaps the best way to describe Goodies is to say that they could just as easily have been named: Misc.

Point to the Goodies menu and pull it down (press the mouse button). Look at the menu options. We already used some of these before by double-clicking the tools they affect. For instance, we looked at the Brush Patterns in Chapter One when we used the Paint Brush. Most of these functions can be turned on in one of two ways: pulling down the menu or double-clicking one of the Tool Box icons.

Goodies
Grid
FatBits
Show Page
Edit Pattern
Brush Shape
Brush Mirrors
Introduction
Short Cuts

This is the Goodies menu

89

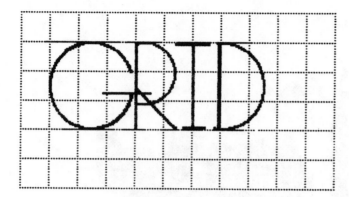

Pull down the Goodies menu until the word Grid is highlighted. Then let go of the mouse button.

| Goodies |
| Grid |
| FatBits |
| Show Page |
| Edit Pattern |
| Brush Shape |
| Brush Mirrors |
| Introduction |
| Short Cuts |

Nothing happened....right? Well, no not exactly. You see, the Grid is a cross between graph paper and an invisible force field. When Grid is on, all of your drawings and paintings will align to invisible lines that are eight dots apart on the screen.

To get an idea of what's going on, get the line tool (＼) and start drawing some horizontal lines on the screen (use the SHIFT key while you draw the lines so they'll come out straight).

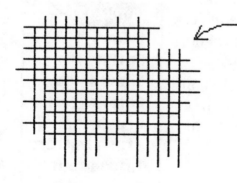

Notice how the cross hairs seem to hesitate and then "pop" into positions on the screen.

If you draw a line in every position that you can, running both horizontally and vertically, you can trace the hidden Grid.

90

Macintosh produces a very high-resolution picture. This means that it uses a whole lot of very small dots on the screen. This is good since it allows us to put a lot of detail in our drawings. The trouble is, these very small dots can be hard to see individually and sometimes we need to be able to make very small changes.

So what shall we do? Buy a magnifying glass?

Nope. MacPaint has a built-in magnifying glass and its called FatBits. FatBits enlarges MacPaint pictures forty-nine (49) times!

Goodies
Grid
FatBits
Show Page
Edit Pattern
Brush Shape
Brush Mirrors
Introduction
Short Cuts

Normal-size bit → □ ■ ← *FatBit*

91

There are three (count'em—three!) ways of turning on FatBits.

1) Pulling down the Goodies menu until the word FatBits is highlighted.
2) Double-clicking the pencil icon (✏).
3) Pressing the ⌘ key while you are in pencil mode (the pencil icon is lit).

So why are there so many ways of turning on FatBits? I'll tell you...I'm not sure. There are some minor differences in the way that they work, however, so perhaps a description of those differences will shed some light on the subject.

First, let's look at the pull-down menu. This is probably the way that you'll use FatBits the most until you get used to using MacPaint. This is primarily because you don't have to memorize anything to use the menu. In fact, you don't even have to remember which menu contains FatBits. Just look through the menus and you'll find it.

To use FatBits from the menu, first draw something on the screen—anything, it really doesn't matter what. Then point at the Goodies menu and press the mouse button. Then pull down until FatBits is lit and let go of the mouse button.

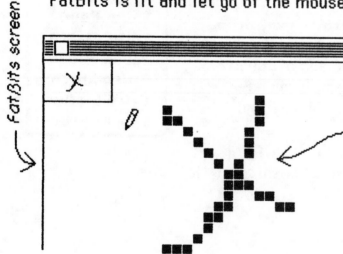

FatBits screen

When FatBits comes on, you'll find that the place that you last did something on the screen (i.e. drew, selected, wrote, filled, etc.) will be in the center of the screen.

When you turn on FatBits by double-clicking, it behaves exactly the same way as it does when you select it from the Goodies menu. The only advantage you'll get from double-clicking is convenience.

On the other hand, pressing the ⌘ key and clicking the mouse (when you are in pencil mode) provides a clear advantage over the other two methods because the FatBits will center in on the exact tip of the pencil point. As a result, you can actually use the pencil to point to any place on the screen and then instantly magnify that point and its surrounding area.

All of the tools work in FatBits. This includes the PaintBrush, Spray Can, Pencil, Line, Circle...everything. The only thing is that since all of the objects in FatBits are forty-nine times larger, you have only one forty-ninth of the screen with which to work.

To compensate for this, MacPaint lets you scroll around the entire work area directly from FatBits. There is (of course) more than one way of scrolling the FatBits screen. The first way is to simply get the grabber (from the tool box) and scroll the screen just as you would the normal (thin-bits) screen. The second method of scrolling in FatBits is to press the Option key (on the keyboard) while you are using the pencil. This will temporarily change the pencil into the grabber and allow you to scroll the screen in any direction.

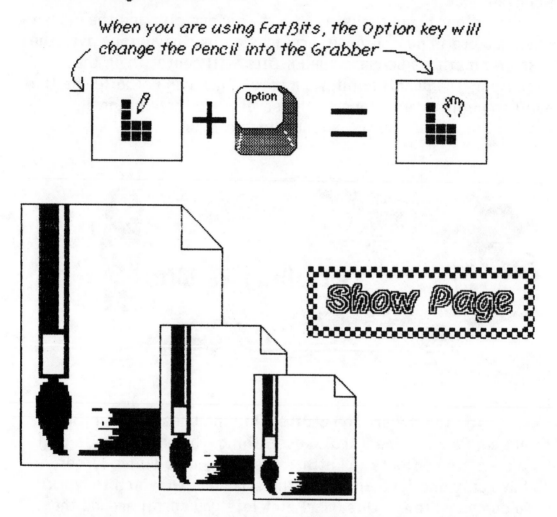

When you are using FatBits, the Option key will change the Pencil into the Grabber

Show Page

Show Page is pretty much the opposite of FatBits (you might call it MiniBits). Although the total work space for MacPaint covers an 8½" x 11" sheet of paper, you can only see a portion of that space at any one time because the Macintosh screen is

94

smaller than that. Show Page reduces the entire MacPaint picture so it can be seen at one time.

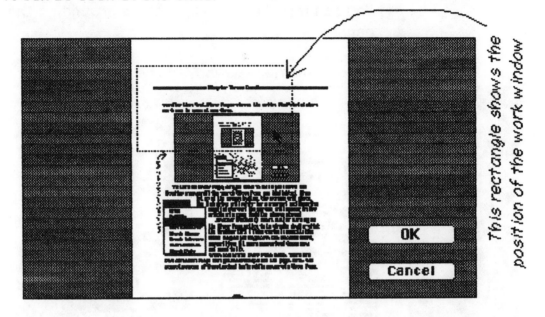

This is how this page looks in Show Page

This rectangle shows the position of the work window

To turn on Show Page, all you need to do is pull down the Goodies menu until the words Show Page are higlighted. Then let go of the mouse button, the screen will clear, the disk drive will whirr for a moment and then the small picture of the screen will appear in the middle of a gray field (as shown above).

Another method (a short cut) of turning on the Show Page option is to simply double-click the Grabber ( ). This works in exactly the same way as pulling down the Goodies menu, except it's a bit more convenient (once you get used to it).

When you are in Show Page mode, there are two different ways that you can manipulate the page. Note: You cannot use any of the standard tools while you are in Show Page.

Goodies
Grid
FatBits
Show Page
Edit Pattern
Brush Shape
Brush Mirrors
Introduction
Short Cuts

The ways that you can manipulate a page are:

1) You can move the work window around on the page.

Here, we've moved the work window down

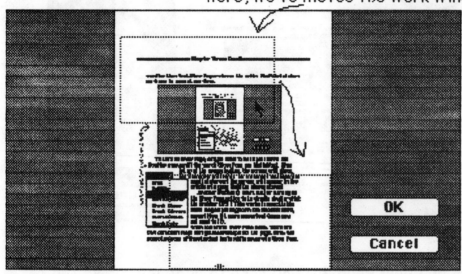

2) We can move the picture around or even right off the page.

Here, part of the picture has been moved up and off the page.

The difference between these two maneuvers is this. When the arrow is pointed inside the rectangle that represents the work area, it will move the rectangle. When the arrow is on the page but outside the work area rectangle, the image on the page moves instead of the rectangle.

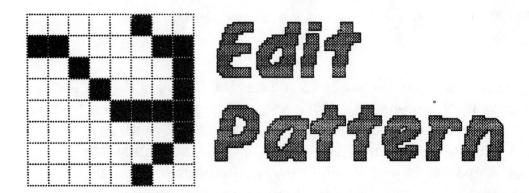

As you probably recall, we edited the palette patterns back in Chapter One. Therefore, there's really no reason to re-hash how it's done. There is one thing, however, that you should know about editing patterns that we didn't cover earlier: You can go into pattern edit mode by just selecting the pattern you want to change and pulling down the Goodies menu to the words Edit Pattern. Other than that, I have nothing to add...except the new pattern that I used in this section's heading...try it out! Note: Just if you forgot how to edit the patterns, the process is covered on pages 36-41 in Chapter One.

Goodies
Grid
FatBits
Show Page
Edit Pattern
Brush Shape
Brush Mirrors
Introduction
Short Cuts

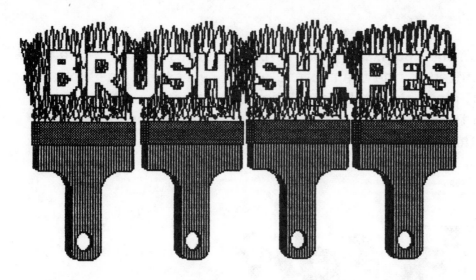

If you look back to pages 7-13 in Chapter One, you'll find that we discussed Brush Shapes before and as I suggested in the last section, we don't need to reupholster subjects we've already covered. So let it suffice to say that you can also access the other brush patterns by pulling down the Goodies menu and stopping at the words Brush Shape. In fact, until you become familiar with MacPaint, this will probably be the easiest way to find these functions.

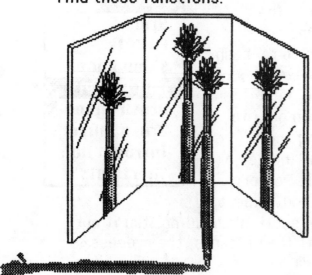

Brush Mirrors

Aha! A subject we haven't covered yet...Brush Mirrors. This option is directly below the Brush Shapes option in the Goodies menu and—believe it or not, there is no short cut to getting them—just the menu.

Pull down the Goodies menu to Brush Mirrors and let go of the mouse button. You should then be presented with the following control window:

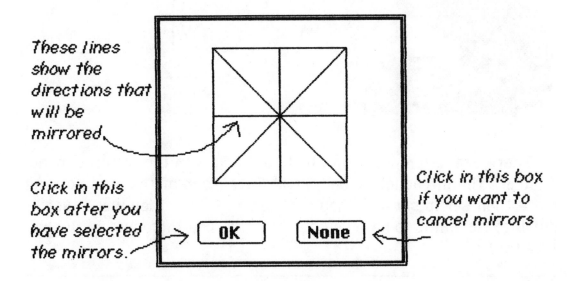

These lines show the directions that will be mirrored.

Click in this box after you have selected the mirrors. → OK

Click in this box if you want to cancel mirrors → None

To select one (or more) of the brush mirrors, just point at the line that indicates the direction you want mirrored and click the mouse button. That line will then darken, indicating that it is selected. To de-select a line, click it again.

Here are some examples of how the Brush Mirrors work:

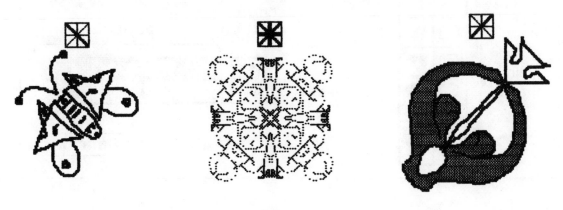

There are two more items left to discuss in the Goodies menu. They are the Introduction and Short Cuts. Each of these is nothing more than a help screen. They don't do anything, they were just put into MacPaint to help you get started. The Introduction looks like this:

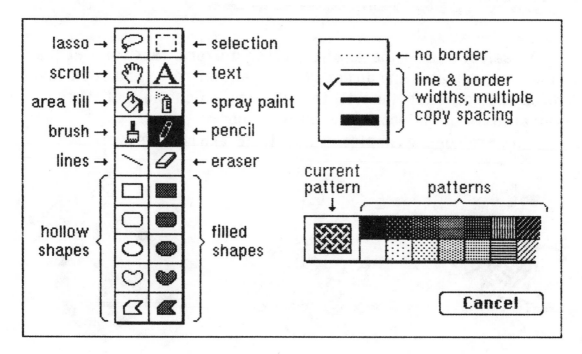

100

The second help screen (Short Cuts) cantains information on how to turn on most of the functions quickly (by double-clicking tools, etc.). After you are done looking at these two screen, in each case, you will need to click on the button that contains the word "Cancel". Doing anything else will produce an error tone.

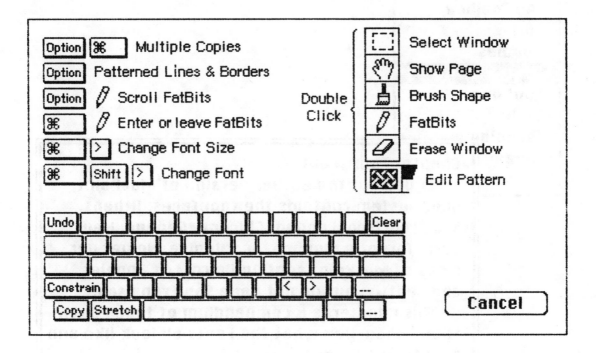

CHAPTER FOUR

Chapter Four: Font

If you got the earlier version of MacPaint, your system contains the typefaces: Athens, San Francisco, London, Chicago, Geneva, New York, Toronto, Monaco, and Venice. Newer versions of MacPaint contain Cairo, Los Angeles, and Seattle, but do not have San Francisco.

This Chapter is a compendium of type Fonts. It will show you what the Fonts all look like and how to use them.

OK

Depending on how you have your system set up, you can have as many as twelve different type fonts at your disposal when you are operating MacPaint. Note: As more fonts become available you can add them to your system if you like. Any way, each of the fonts can have as many as 188 characters...with 12 fonts that means you can get 2,256 different characters! Now look at the keyboard. It only has 47 character keys (the rest are function keys such as SHIFT, RETURN, TAB, etc.). To get all 188 different characters, you must use various combinations of SHIFT and the Option key.

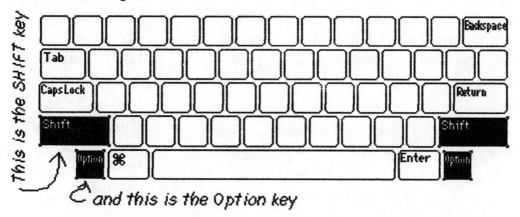

This is the SHIFT key

and this is the Option key

Notice that the keyboard has two Option Keys and two SHIFT keys. The extra keys are for convenience only. You need only press one of them (one of the keys marked SHIFT, one of the keys marked Option or one of each) depending on the function you want to get.

Each of the keyboard diagrams in this chapter is pictured with either no keys highlighted, the SHIFT keys highlighted, the Option keys highlighted, or both the SHIFT and OPTION keys highlighted. Depending on which keys are highlighted, you'll need to press one or more of them to get the characters that are displayed on the keyboard diagram to print. Use the diagrams as a guide for this purpose.

To select one of the Fonts, point the arrow at the Font menu, press the mouse button and pull down until the Font you want is highlighted, then let go of the mouse button.

Notice that this Font menu contains all of the Fonts that are currently available on the Macintosh. It is actually not a very good idea to keep all of them in the file at once because the take up a lot of disk space. It is much better to select a few Fonts and put those on your MacPaint disk, saving the rest of them on another disk so you can access them later.

This menu shows all of the current Fonts. Depending on your system, you will probably not have (or want) all of these at one time.

Font
Toronto
Athens
San Francisco
London
Cairo
Los Angeles
Seattle
Chicago
✓Geneva
New York
Monaco
Venice

Note: In the keyboard diagrams that follow, most of the characters are shown in 18 point (the FontSize—see the next chapter for more information about FontSize). However, in some cases, the 18 point characters did not fit well in the keyboard diagram. In those cases, the characters were enlarged or reduced to fit. For a complete chart of all the character sizes, see chapter five.

Athens

Note: Some of the characters in the Option character sets are accent marks. To use them, press the key that has the accent mark (`, ´, ¨, etc.) and then the letter that should go below it.

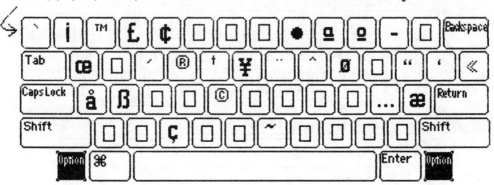

Athens...(continued)

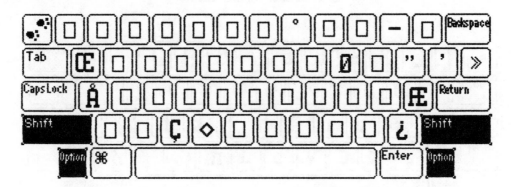

San Francisco

San Francisco...(continued)

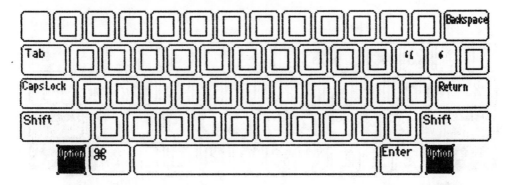

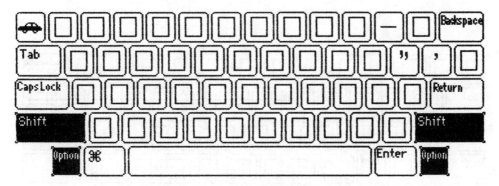

London

London...(continued)

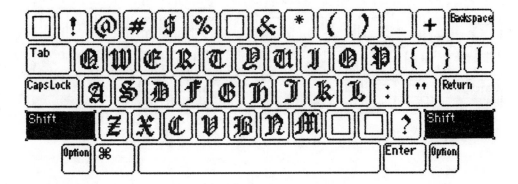

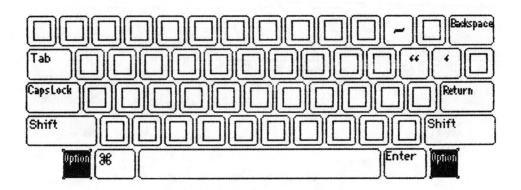

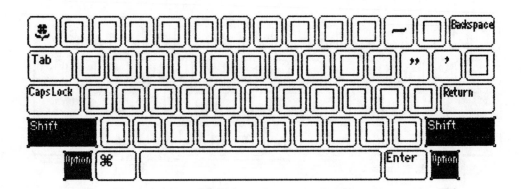

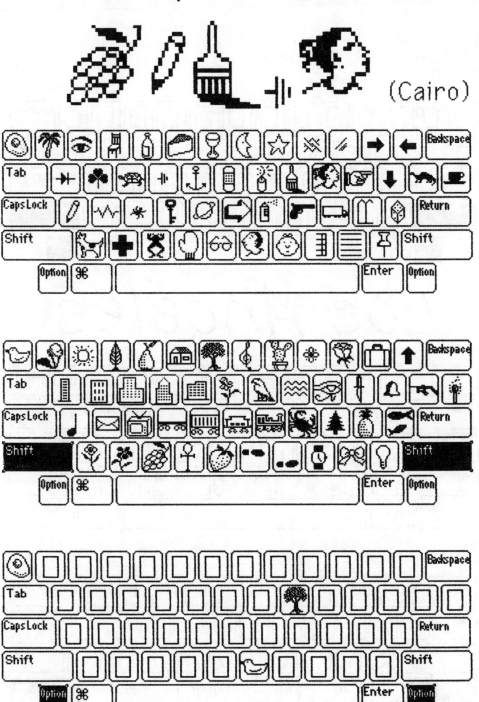

(Cairo)

...(continued)

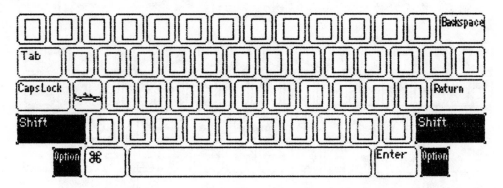

Los Angeles

Los Angeles...(continued)

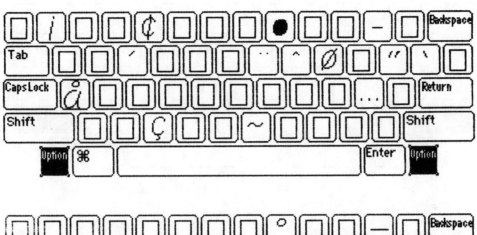

Seattle

111

Seattle...(continued)

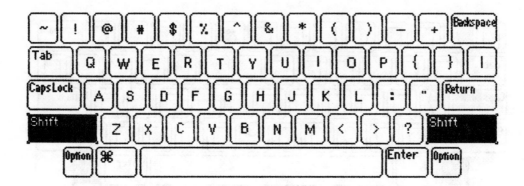

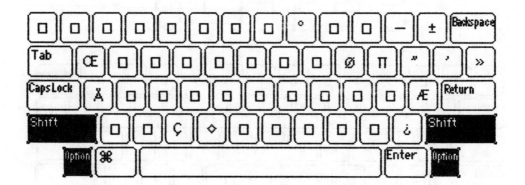

Chicago

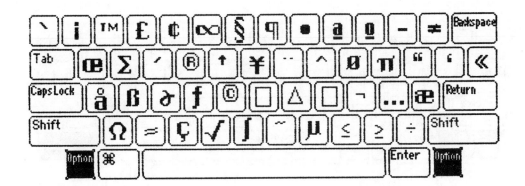

Chicago...(continued)

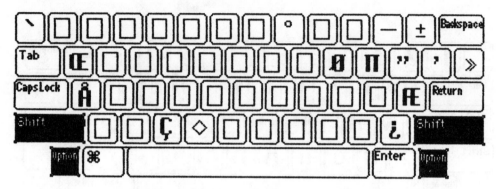

Geneva

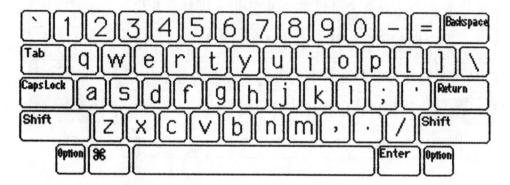

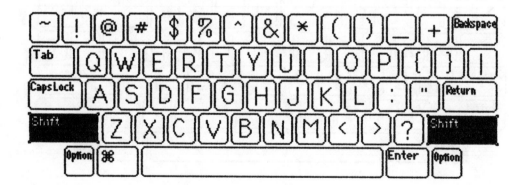

Geneva...(continued)

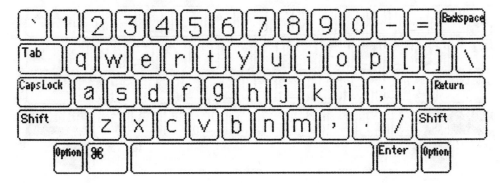

New York

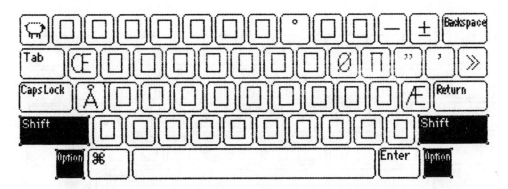

New York...(continued)

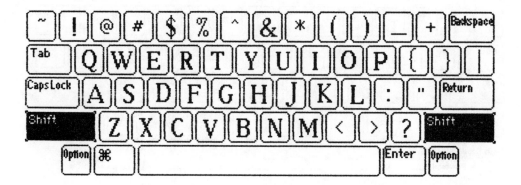

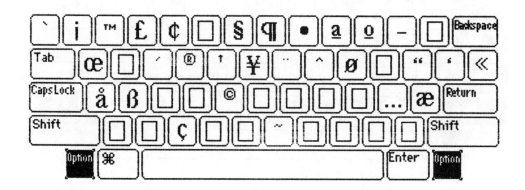

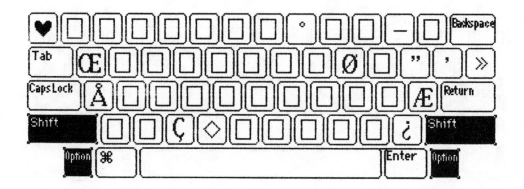

Monaco

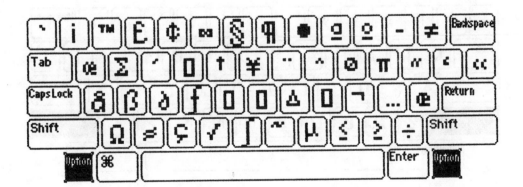

Monaco...(continued)

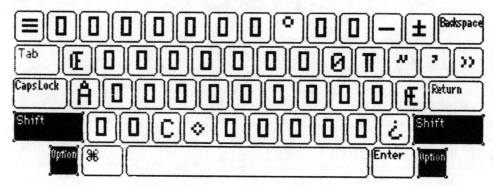

Venice

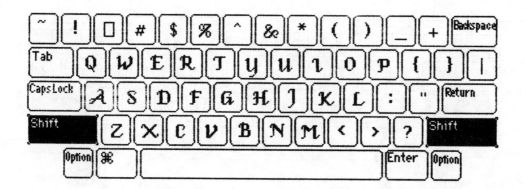

Venice...(continued)

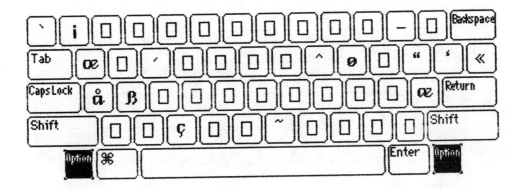

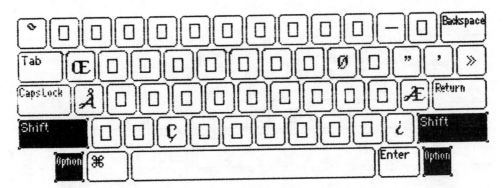

Toronto

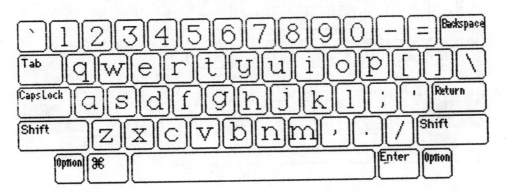

Toronto...(continued)

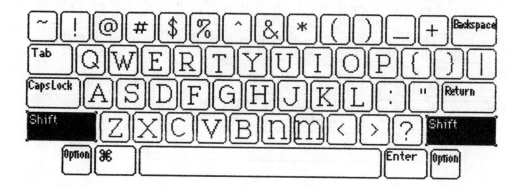

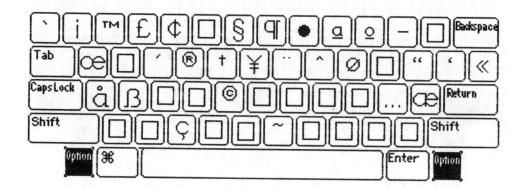

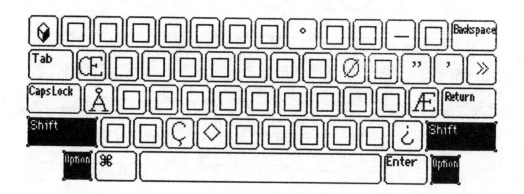

There's LESS to this than meets the EYE.

If you look back at the character sets in this chapter, you see that not all of the 2,256 characters are different. In fact, 666 of them are boxes of various shapes. That leaves 1,590 different characters – still a tidy number.

In the next chapter we'll discuss FontSize. MacPaint can make the characters both larger and smaller than the ones we've used in this chapter – nine different sizes in all. That means that our 1,590 characters become 14,310 characters.

Interested? ... Then read on ☞ (Cairo, 18 pt)

CHAPTER FIVE

Contents

Introduction

The Toolbox
Edit
Goodies
Font
FontSize
Style
Techniques
Index
Finder

Chapter Five: FontSize
    In the last chapter we looked at the twelve different Fonts that MacPaint can use. In this chapter we'll cover all of the different sizes MacPaint can produce, how they are produced, and how to make the best use of them. Additionally, we'll look at MacPaint's hidden character set(s) and how Fontsize is the key to them all.

OK

In the last chapter, we discussed the Fonts (shapes of all the characters). In this chapter we'll look at size. For MacPaint, the characters don't just get larger or smaller, their shapes must be recalculated each time they change size. As a result of this, some of the character sizes look better than others... but enough with these generalities! Let's look at the characters themselves.

Fontmover Revisited

Pull down the FontSize window (point at it with the arrow and press the mouse button). There are nine options in this menu. They are: 9 point, 12, 14, 18, 24, 36, 48, and 72. So what—you may ask—is a point? A point is a printing term that refers to the height of a character. Each point is 1/72 of an inch. So, for example, a 1 point Font would have letters that are 1/72" tall.

These two W's are each shown in 36 point. This means that they are 1/2" tall. As you can see, stacked one on top of the other, they make an inch.

½ inch
½ inch

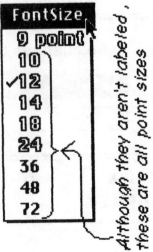

FontSize
9 point
10
✓12
14
18
24
36
48
72

Although they aren't labeled, these are all point sizes

Now take a look at the FontSize menu itself. See how some of the numbers are outlined (9 point, 10, 12, 14, 18, and 24) while the other numbers (36, 48, and 72) are printed in plain type. The numbers that are outlined are stored in memory exactly the way that you see them—in the same size as shown. On the other hand the FontSizes that are plain are not stored in memory at all. To produce those sizes, MacPaint looks at the closest FontSize to the one selected and calculates the shape of the one you want. To get a better idea of how this works, we'll need to take another look at Font Mover—the program that we used earlier to remove the Fonts that we wouldn't be needing with MacPaint.

If you are currently in MacPaint, exit the program by pulling down the File menu and pointing to the work Quit.

| File |
| **New** |
| **Open...** |
| Close |
| Save |
| Save As... |
| Revert |
| Print Draft |
| Print Final |
| **Print Catalog** |
| Quit |

To exit MacPaint, pull down to Quit.

Note: If you did not save the current picture before selecting Quit, MacPaint will present you with the following message box:

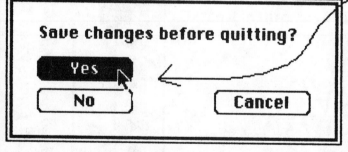

Save changes before quitting?

Yes

No   Cancel

Click on Yes if you want to save the picture.

If you don't want to save the picture, click No and MacPaint will simply exit.

Cancel returns you to MacPaint.

After a bit of whirring and buzzing you should be looking at the desk top. Using the methods we covered earlier, find the Font Mover program.

NOTE: If you cannot find the Font Mover program on the current disk (the one that has MacPaint on it) look at the System disk that came with Macintosh, it should have Font Mover on it.

To look at another disk, you'll need to first eject the current disk by either pulling down the File menu to the word Eject or by pressing the ⌘ key, the SHIFT key and the 1 key. This will eject the disk from drive one (the internal drive). If you have an extra disk drive (external drive) press ⌘, SHIFT and the 2 key.

File

Open
Duplicate   ⌘D
Get Info   ⌘I
Put Back

Close
Close All
Print

Eject   ⌘E

If you want to eject disk one (in the internal drive) you can press ⌘, SHIFT, and the one key.

If find the Font Mover program on another disk, you'll need to make a copy of it on the MacPaint disk for this example.

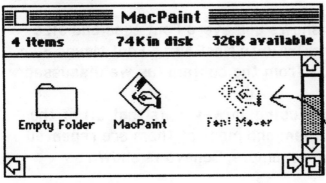

MacPaint

4 items   74K in disk   326K available

Empty Folder   MacPaint   Font Mover

To copy Font Mover, point the arrow at the icon Font Mover and drag it over to the MacPaint disk window

Font Mover

The reason that Font Mover must be on the MacPaint disk is that Font Mover can only manipulate Fonts that are on the same disk that it is on.

Double-click the Font Mover icon on the MacPaint disk. The screen should go blank for a few moments, but after a bit of whirring and clicking you should see this window:

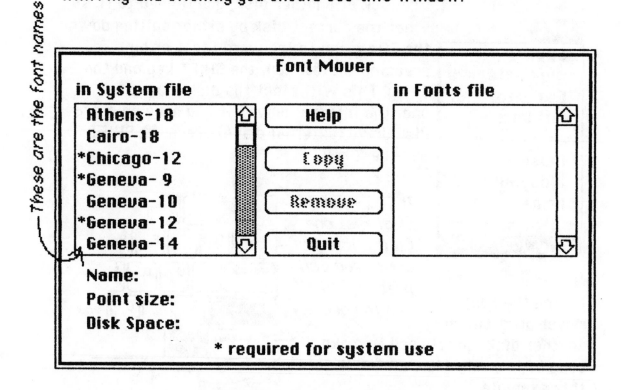

The Font Mover window shows you every Font type and size currently in the system (available to MacPaint). Font Mover also lets you add or remove fonts from the system (as we discussed earlier on in this book).

One thing that may be confusing, however, is that all of the fonts have numbers beside them and most of them are repeated (except for the numbers). For example, Geneva is shown as

Geneva-9, Geneva-10, Geneva-12, and Geneva-14. The numbers that follow the font names are font sizes (9 point, 10 point, etc.) and the asterisks to the left of the names indicate that you should not use Font Mover to remove them because Macintosh needs them to operate (print messages, disk and file names, and so on).

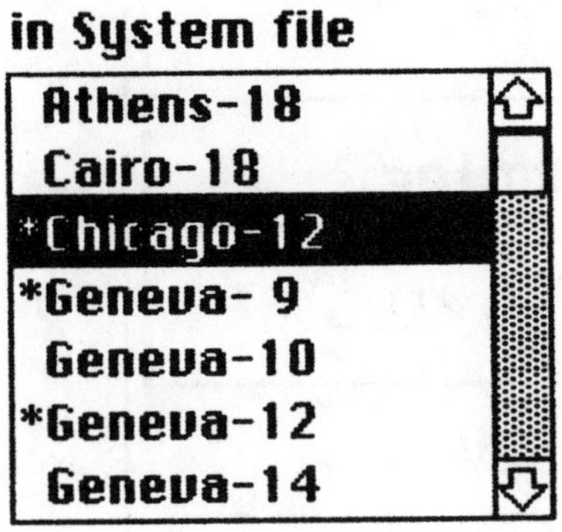

in System file

Athens-18	⬆
Cairo-18	
*Chicago-12	
*Geneva- 9	
Geneva-10	
*Geneva-12	
Geneva-14	⬇

Now let's take a look at the left hand window of the Font Mover. If we select one of the fonts (by pointing the arrow at it and clicking the mouse button) it will highlight and some additional information about that font will appear below the window. In the example at the left, we've selected Chicago-12.

Name: Chicago-12

Point size: 12   **Sample**

Disk Space: 2940

In this case, the additional information is that Chicago-12 is the name of the font, it is a 12 point font it occupies 2940 bytes of disk space and the word sample shows how it looks. Note: Because Chicago is the system font that Font Mover uses, all of the text (in this case) is printed in Chicago.

Now select some of the other fonts by clicking on them. You'll find that Geneva-9, for example, requires only 2152 of disk space while Geneva-14 needs more than 3500 bytes. The larger a font size, the more disk space it requires.

Now take a look at the scroll bar that runs along the right edge of the "in System file" window. It's gray and, like any other gray scroll bar, it allows you to "scroll" within the window. In

127

this case you can use the scroll bar to look at all of the fonts in the system. At the time of this printing, the fonts and font sizes available are:

Font Name	Space
Athens-18	**4468 bytes**
 (Cairo-18)	5840 bytes
Chicago-12	**2940 bytes**
Geneva-9	2152 bytes
Geneva-10	2200 bytes
Geneva-12	2734 bytes
Geneva-14	3568 bytes
Geneva-18	4864 bytes
Geneva-20	5848 bytes
Geneva-24	7568 bytes

Continued ➡

128

Font Name	Space
London-18	3268 bytes
Los Angeles-12	2440 bytes
Los Angeles-24	6440 bytes
Monaco-9	2026 bytes
Monaco-12	2464 bytes
New York-9	2032 bytes
New York-10	2200 bytes
New York-12	2734 bytes
New York-14	3352 bytes
New York-18	4516 bytes
New York-20	5260 bytes
New York-24	6832 bytes
New York-36	13780 bytes

More ➡

Font Name	Space
San Francisco-18	2984 Bytes
Seattle-10	2410 Bytes
Seattle-20	6302 bytes
Toronto-9	2308 bytes
Toronto-12	3034 bytes
Toronto-14	3658 bytes
Toronto-18	5688 bytes
Toronto-24	8854 bytes
Venice-14	3604 bytes

There you are—that's all of the fonts currently available on MacPaint. If you look at the fonts on this chart, you'll find three fonts that you cannot get to from MacPaint: Geneva-20, New York-20 and Seattle-20. That's because MacPaint doesn't let you use 20 point fonts.

Now, let's look at the different FontSize menus again. In each case, some of the font sizes are shown in outlined type while others are shown in plain type. If you look at these closely, you'll find that these correspond directly with the font sizes that are in the system.

130

from MacPaint

FontSize

9 point
10
✓12
14
18
24
36
48
72

The FontSize menu on the left corresponds to the font sizes available with the New York font. If you look back at the FontSize chart (pages 128 through 130) you'll find that New York is stored in 9, 10, 12, 14, 18, 20, 24, and 36 point. Note: Just a reminder: 20 point type is not available in MacPaint.

Now look at the menu; 9 point, 10, 12, 14, 18, 24, and 36 are printed in outlined numbers. These are the same type sizes we found in the chart. Note: The chart lists all of the font sizes listed in Font Mover.

One question that arises from all of this is "Why would there be so many different sizes of each font—after all, MacPaint can simply calculate the shapes of different size fonts and every extra font (expecially the larger ones) takes up valuable disk space?"

The answer is this: When MacPaint enlarges or reduces a font, there is a noticeable loss in the quality of the printing. For example, let's see what happens to New York if we remove all of the New York font sizes except ... New York 18 (which is near to the middle size).

If you have left Font Mover to look at the MacPaint examples above, return to Font Mover again (as we did earlier) and look at the control buttons in the center of the Font Mover window. There are four buttons in the center of the window: Help, Copy, Remove, and Quit.

Help is a short description of how Font Mover works and Quit will exit Font Mover. The other two buttons (Copy and Remove are the ones we'll use to delete the New York fonts in this experiment.

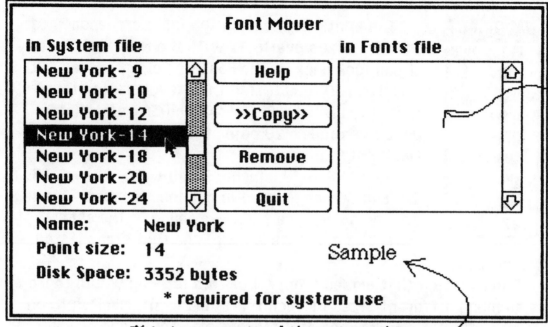

Font Mover

in System file   **in Fonts file**

New York- 9
New York-10
New York-12
New York-14
New York-18
New York-20
New York-24

Help

>>Copy>>

Remove

Quit

Name: New York
Point size: 14
Disk Space: 3352 bytes

Sample

* **required for system use**

This is a sample of the selected Font

When you click Copy, the Font will appear in the "In Fonts File" window.

To remove a font, select it (by pointing the arrow at it and clicking the mouse button) and then click on the Remove button. Note: If you want to put the fonts back after we're done, click on the Copy button first (this will place a copy of the font you're removing in a separate Fonts file).

Once you have removed all of the New York fonts except New York-18, Quit Font Mover and return to MacPaint (click on the Quit button and after you return to the desk top, double-click on the MacPaint icon.

To return to MacPaint, double-click the MacPaint icon.

MacPaint

4 items   **74K in disk**   **326K available**

Empty Folder   MacPaint   Font Mover

Before we try typing any text, let's take a look at the New York FontSize window to see if it has changed, now that we only have New York-18 available on the disk.

As you can see, the window is quite different. Now the only point size that is printed in outlined letters is 18 point. All the others are shown in plain type.

Now let's see how different the type itself looks (as MacPaint calculates the different sizes).

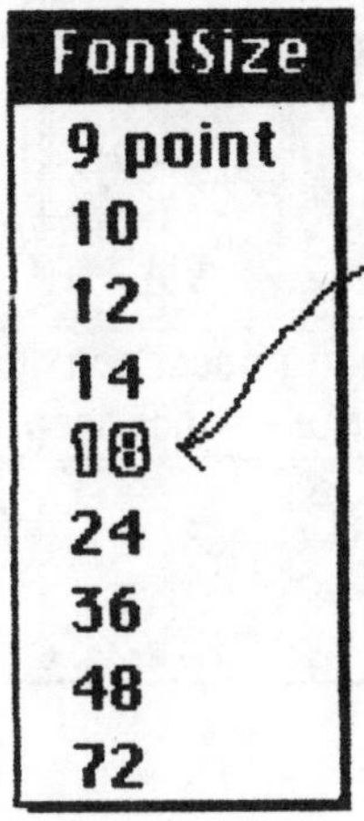

The chart below shows New York 9, 10, 12, 14, 24, and 36 as it looked before (with those fonts in memory) and now (with only New York in memory).

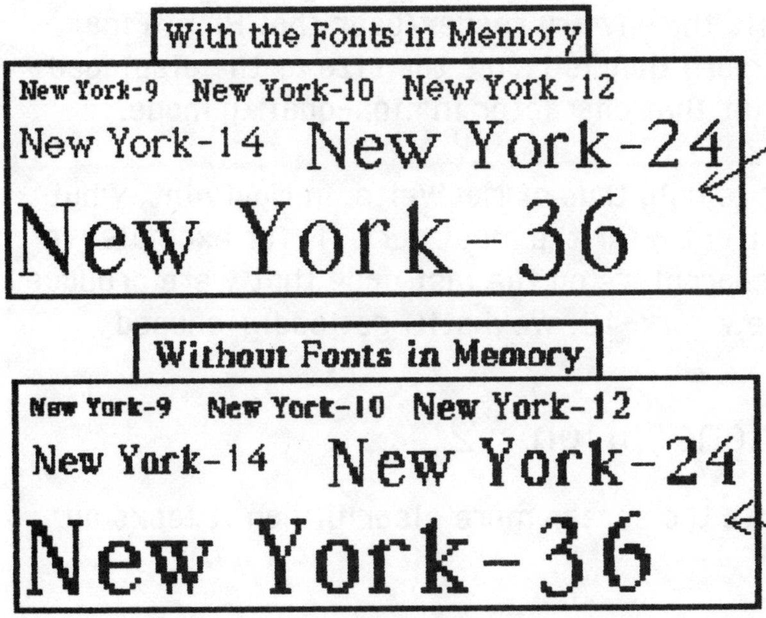

FontSize

9 point
10
12
14
18
24
36
48
72

New York-18 is the only font size left on the disk.

With the Fonts in Memory

New York-9   New York-10   New York-12
New York-14   New York-24
New York-36

Without Fonts in Memory

New York-9   New York-10   New York-12
New York-14   New York-24
New York-36

As you can see, the characters printed with the actual font sizes in memory are much clearer than the characters that MacPaint calculates.

Common Misconception #1:

Somewhere in the Macintosh documentation, there is a statement that tells the unwary reader/user that Print Final needs a font in memory that is twice the size of the displayed font in order to print that character in high-quality mode.

Wrong!

That statement is only true of MacWrite. In MacPaint, what you see is what you get—for the most part. If, for example we were to print the characters on the last page that were produced by recalculating New York-18, we'd still get oddly-shaped characters.

Common Misconception #2:

Print Final prints the screen more clearly than it looks on the Macintosh.

Wrong again.

Print Final Prints more dots than the Macintosh screen, but it does not provide better resolution. The way Final Print works is this:

Normally (in Draft Print) the Imagewriter (the Macintosh printer) prints a single dot on the paper for every dot that appears on the Macintosh screen. Therefore Draft mode produces a picture that is precisely the same as the screen—with only one exception: the Imagewriter dots are round while the Macintosh screen dots are square.

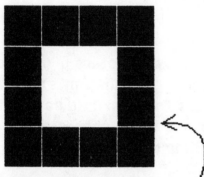

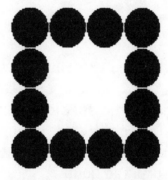

Enlarged picture of a square as displayed on the Mac screen.

The same square, printed in Draft mode by the Apple Imagewriter printer.

In Final Print mode, the image writer prints each row of dots twice, spacing about a half dot height between each of the print passes.

By printing between the rows of dots, Final Print tends to fill in the ragged gaps between the dots.

These dots were printed on the first pass.

These were printed on the second pass.

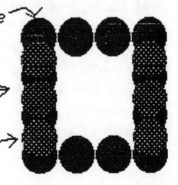

Hidden Fonts

In addition to printing the standard characters you see on the keyboards (look back in chapter four for all the fonts), Macintosh has also got some special characters that can only be accessed by switching font sizes. In some cases these characters are just larger or smaller pictures of the same object, but in some cases they can surprise you.

To print the hidden characters, press the SHIFT key, the Option key and the key in the upper left-hand corner of the keyboard ⌐. Then, depending on which character set and font size you're using, you'll get one of these characters:

> **NOTE: If you want to simply explore all of the different characters you can get using different fonts and font sizes, you need only type one character and then, just change fonts and/or font sizes by either pulling down your menu choices, or by pressing ⌘ and the > key to select larger fonts or the < key to select smaller fonts. The key combination of ⌘ , SHIFT and > (or <) will cycle through all of the type styles.**

136

The Special Characters

POINT SIZE	TORONTO	ATHENS	SAN FRANCISCO
9			
10			
12			
14			
18			
24			
36			
48			
72			

The Special Characters

P O I N T S I Z E	LONDON	CAIRO	LOS ANGELES
9	⚘	□	□
10	⚘	□	□
12	⚘	□	□
14	⚘	□	□
18	⚘	□	□
24	⚘	□	□
36	⚘	□	□
48	⚘	□	□
72	⚘	□	□

The Special Characters

POINT SIZE	SEATTLE	CHICAGO	GENEVA
9	□	□	
10	□	□	
12	□	□	
14	□	□	
18	□	□	
24	□	□	
36	□	□	
48	□	□	
72	□	□	

139

The Special Characters

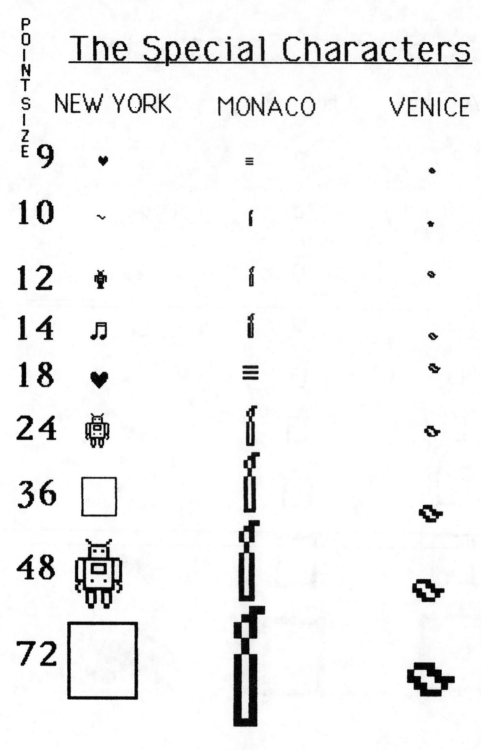

This concludes our discussion on FontSize. If we add the 70 new characters (this does not include the assortment of boxes) that were hidden within the keyboard we are now up to 14,380 different characters in the Macintosh. However, we're still not finished. In the next chapter, we'll discuss Style. Style is another function that modifies the Macintosh characters (like FontSize).

Of course, I don't want to give away any hints about the next chapter, but when you're done, you'll know how to produce almost half a million different characters.

So why are you wasting your time reading the conclusion to this chapter—this is old stuff. Turn the page!

CHAPTER SIX

Contents

Chapter Six: Style

In the previous two chapters, we looked at the different character sets that MacPaint has at its disposal. We also looked at one way of modifying the characters in those fonts* by making them larger or smaller.

In this chapter, you"l learn how to modify them even more drastically—and with (ahem)... Style.

OK

*A font is a character set.

142

STYLE

If you look to the menu headings, you'll find that the last one (on the right) is called Style. Style lets you change any of the characters in any of the fonts by making those characters Bold, Italic, Underlined, Outlined, or Shadowed. Style also lets you align the characters to the left, to the right or in the center.

In the last two chapters, all of the characters in all of the fonts we looked at were (in terms of style) Plain. Plain is the first item in the Style menu—it's a lot like a reset switch. However, before I go off into an explanation of how to reset anything, let's just say that whenever you select Plain, that's what you'll get—plain characters with none of the special style features.

Style	
✓Plain	⌘P
Bold	⌘B
Italic	⌘I
Underline	⌘U
Outline	⌘O
Shadow	⌘S
✓Align Left	⌘L
Align Middle	⌘M
Align Right	⌘R

The Style menu

Character Alignment

Although character alignment is not the first option in the Style menu, it is the simplest function and as such, it should be the first of the Style options we discuss.

The Insertion Point

If you look back to page 62, you'll find that we discussed a MacPaint pointer called the I-beam. When you are in character mode (ie. the [A] icon is highlighted), you can select an insertion point (the place where Mac will start printing characters) by simply moving the I-beam around on the screen. When you have found the place you want to begin typing, just click the mouse button and the I-beam will be replaced by a vertical bar.

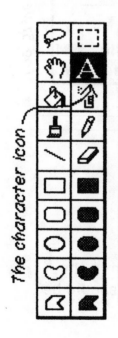

The character icon

This is the insertion point.

I ←

This is the I-Beam.

Once you have positioned the insertion point, you can move the I-Beam again and as long as you do not click the mouse button, the insertion point will not move (except to follow any text you enter).

144

Up until now, whenever we entered text in MacPaint, we entered it in Align Left mode. In other words, all of the lines of text lined up along the left margin.

Style	
✓Plain	⌘P
Bold	⌘B
Italic	⌘I
<u>Underline</u>	⌘U
Outline	⌘O
Shadow	⌘S
✓Align Left	⌘L
Align Middle	⌘M
Align Right	⌘R

Pull down the Style menu (point the arrow at the menu heading and press the mouse button) and you will see that Align Left (the third item from the bottom of the menu) is checked. Note: In the menu at left, it is also highlighted as it would be if you pulled down to that point with the arrow.

Actually, you don't have to select Align Left initially because it is the default selection (made by MacPaint for you).

Let's take a look at some examples of text that is aligned to the left margin.

Little Bo Peep has
lost her sheep and doesn't
know where to find them

Jack and Jill went up the hill
to fetch a pail of water.
Jack fell down and broke
his crown and Jill came
tumbling after

Notice that in each of the two sections of text above, the left-hand edge of the lines of text all line up. In Align Left mode each

145

time you type a character, the character is aligned to the right of the insertion point and the insertion point is then moved to the right of the character awaiting another key stroke.

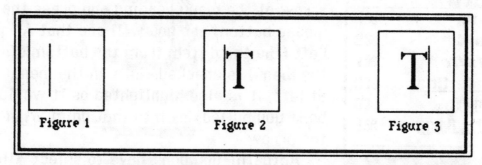

Figure 1   Figure 2   Figure 3

Figure 1 (above) shows the insertion point (36 point size) before any characters have been typed. In Figure 2, we have typed the letter "T." Note: Ordinarily, the insertion point disappears as soon as we type a character—it is shown here simply for reference. In Figure 3, we see that the insertion point has now moved to a position to the right of the letter "T."

Align right is similar to align left, but (as you probably guessed) it lines up the characters to the right margin. By the way, in case you haven't figured it out yet, the margin (when you are using Align Left or Align Right) is set by the position of the I-Beam when you select the insertion point.

To select Align Right, pull down the Style menu and keep pulling down until the words Align Right are highlighted. Note: Look at the menu options in this menu. Notice that all of them have the ⌘ symbol followed by a letter in the right-hand column. By pressing the ⌘ key and the indicated letter, you can switch from one menu item to another without pulling down this menu.

Alternate selection keys

Style	
✓Plain	⌘P
Bold	⌘B
Italic	⌘I
Underline	⌘U
Outline	⌘O
Shadow	⌘S
Align Left	⌘L
Align Middle	⌘M
✓Align Right	⌘R

Align Right

146

Four score and
seven years ago
Our Fathers
brought forth
Upon this
Continent,
A new nation

In the example above, the insertion point was placed just to the left of the upper left-hand corner of the flag. That way, as letters were typed, they were pushed off to the left of the insertion point.

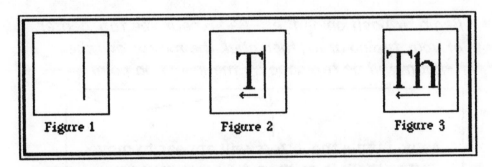

Figure 1   Figure 2   Figure 3

As with Align Left, Figure 1 shows the insertion point, just before any characters have been typed (Align Right mode.) Figure 2 shows a capital "T" being typed and pushed out to the left of the insertion point. Finally, in Figure 3, we see yet another letter (a lower case "h") typed next to the "T" pushes them both to the left . Since the insertion point is always at the extreme right of the line, a carriage return (pressing RETURN) simply moves the insertion point down (not to the left).

The last of the three alignment options is Align Middle. Align Middle splits the width of each character in two and moves the character half a width to the left while it moves the insertion point the same distance to the right.

Since align middle is the most difficult of the alignment modes to understand and master, let's begin by setting it up and typing a few lines.

To select Align Middle, either pull down the Style menu until the words Align Middle are highlighted or press ⌘ and M on the keyboard.

Now, put the I-Beam somewhere in the top and middle of the area in which you want to type and click the mouse button.

Style	
✓Plain	⌘P
Bold	⌘B
Italic	⌘I
Underline	⌘U
Outline	⌘O
Shadow	⌘S
Align Left	⌘L
✓Align Middle	⌘M
Align Right	⌘R

Begin by positioning the I-Beam near the top, center of your typing area, then click the mouse and the I-Beam will be replaced by the insertion point

As you type, the letters will appear to move
off to the left, as they did when you were
using Align Right, but if you
look closely, you'll see that the insertion
point is moving off to the right at
same rate that the letters are
moving off to the left.

148

To get a better idea of how this works, let's take a look at the progression of the characters as they are typed.

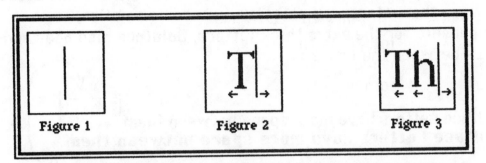

Figure 1   Figure 2   Figure 3

In this third example we find that Align Middle causes both the letters and the insertion point to move away from the center of the text. Figure 1 shows the inserion point in the center of the typing area. In Figure 2 we have typed a "T" which has been pushed to the left of center while the insertion point has been pushed exactly the same distance but to the right. In Figure 3 we have typed the letter "h" and both the "T" and the "h" have moved left while the insertion point has once again moved the same distance to the right.

BOLDFACE

The second option in the Style menu (right below Plain) is called Boldface. Boldface takes a plain character and doubles the width of the horizontal lines and spaces. To get a clearer idea of this, take a look at the illustration below.

As you can see, the vertical lines in the letter are the same

On the other hand, the vertical lines are thicker.

So as you can see, the vertical lines (the ones that run up and down) become twice as thick while the horizontal lines stay the same. Of course, if we make the letters thicker, then the spaces between the letters will effectively become smaller, so to compensate for the extra thick letters, Boldface also adds some space between the letters.

Boldface Letters have more space between them.
Boldface Letters have more space between them.

As you can see from this sentence, the boldface letters make a longer sentence.

Italics

The next Style option is Italics. Italics simply "leans" the characters to the right a bit. In this case, a "bit" is actually (if you want to get technical) 22½° to the right. However, as the old Chinese proverb says (I think it's Chinese...) "One picture is worth 1,000 words."

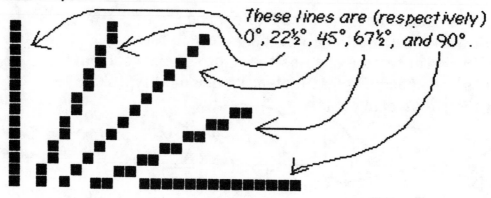

These lines are (respectively) 0°, 22½°, 45°, 67½°, and 90°.

Based on this $22\frac{1}{2}°$ degree slant then, here are some examples of characters, both plain and italic:

PLAIN	ITALIC
Toronto	Toronto
London	London

Style

✓Plain	⌘P
✓Bold	⌘B
✓ Italic	⌘I
Underline	⌘U
Outline	⌘O
Shadow	⌘S
✓Align Left	⌘L
Align Middle	⌘M
Align Right	⌘R

Oh, by the way, I almost forgot... each time that you are done using one of the options in the Style menu, like Bold or Italic, you need to reset that function or you'll still be using it later. To reset the Style functions you can either re-select them (i.e. point the arrow at the item from the menu or press the ⌘ key and the appropriate letter) or (as I mentioned at the beginning of this section), select Plain (which will reset all of the Style options).

If you only want to rest some of the Style options but don't know which have been selected, look at the menu. Each of the options that is currently selected will have a small check mark beside it. If you de-select that item, the check mark will disappear.

151

A little bit about:

Underline

and a lot about using Style

Okay, here's the scoop about Underline. You can select it from the menu or by pressing ⌘ and U. If you select it, MacPaint will draw a very neat little line right under all of the characters that you type—as you type them. (Ho-humm...z..z.z.zzzzz). Not real exciting—right? But very useful so don't forget how to use it.

Now, about using Style. I had a lot of extra room here because I didn't have a lot to say about Underline so I thought that this was as good a time as any to cover a small "feature" about Style that is both wonderful and a pain in the .... neck. If you are typing a section of text, that section of text will be treated as a unit and any changes that you make to part of it will happen to the rest of it...even if you don't want that—especially if you don't want that!

To get a better idea of what I'm complaining about, let's enter a small block of text:

The quick brown
fox jumped over
the lazy dog's
back.

This is the way that the block was originally entered

The quick brown
fox jumped over
the lazy dog's
back.

Here, I wanted to underline the word "back." Instead, everything was underlined

152

Try this for yourself: Type in the sentence on the previous page using MacPaint. Now, before you type in the last word in the block ("back"), select the Underline option from Style. Oops! All of the letters in the block are suddenly underlined. Now, this can be a real nice feature if you enter an entire block of text and then, after entering it, you decide that you want it to be printed in larger characters, a different font, underlined or whatever. However, if you want to insert a single word that is underlined or bold, you need to stop the current block and start a new one by repositioning the insertion point with the I-Beam and clicking the mouse button.

Outline

Outline is right below the Underline option in the Style menu. You can select it just as you do any of the other Style options. You can either: pull down the menu until the word Outline is highlighted or simply press the ⌘ key and "O" on the keyboard.

Outlined letters are very similar to shapes that are produced using the Trace Edges option from the Edit menu with just one or two minor differences. Let's take a look at how Outline and Trace Edges differ:

Style	
✓Plain	⌘P
Bold	⌘B
Italic	⌘I
Underline	⌘U
Outline	⌘O
Shadow	⌘S
✓Align Left	⌘L
Align Middle	⌘M
Align Right	⌘R

Of course, the best way to "see" the difference between Trace Edges and Outline is to see the difference. The two words below were written identically but the word on the right was outlined using the Outline option from the Style menu and the word on the left was outlined using Trace Edges from the Edit menu.

Outlined using
Trace Edges

Outlined using
the Outline option

As you can see, in this example, the differences between Outline and Trace Edges are minimal. Now, let's look at how these appear using larger letters.

Outlined using
Trace Edges

Outlined using
Outline

With larger letters, one of the differences between Outline and Trace Edges becomes apparent: Outline uses lines that become thicker to correspond to the size of the letters being outlined while Trace Edges always uses thin lines.

There is yet another difference between Trace Edges and Outline: Outline always follows the shape of the characters,

154

if you use Trace Edges multiple times, it will start following its own edges and will soon make the character un-readable.

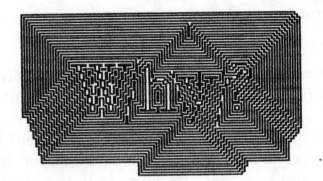

...Why?

Shadow is similar to Outline, but instead of outlining the edges of the character, Shadow puts a "weighted" border around the character that looks like a shadow.

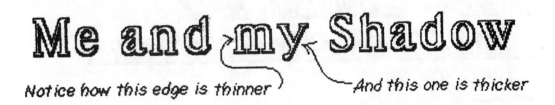

Notice how this edge is thinner   *And this one is thicker*

Mixing and Matching

Okay folks, here's the last piece of information you'll get about MacPaint before we go into the chapter on MacPaint Techniques.

In addition to being able to use each of the different Style options alone, you can use them in combination. So for example, you can produce characters that are Bold and Outlined or Underlined Italics. Any combination that you can think of will work (except Plain—Plain just means that all of the options are turned off).

Plain   **Bold**

<u>Underlined</u>   *Italics*

Outlined   **Shadowed**

<u>**Bold/Underlined**</u>   *Outlined Italics*

Bold/Shadowed/ Outlined/Underlined Italics

CHAPTER
SEVEN

Chapter Seven: Techniques

So far in this book, we've covered all of the things that MacPaint can do, like making lines and squares, typing letters and adding patterns.

Throughout the book, you've also seen lots of drawings that were made with MacPaint. As a matter of fact, the entire book including the text and all the pictures were drawn using MacPaint.

In this chapter, you'll learn how it was done.

OK

A few More

Although we've covered all of the MacPaint tools and functions and we've looked at the way that they all interact, there are still a few functions that we haven't seen. That's because they aren't MacPaint functions—they are Macintosh functions. The point is— MacPaint can use them and do some very special things with some of them. And some of them are important because we can use them as aids when we use MacPaint.

Saving the Screen

If you look through this book, you'll see lots of pictures of Macintosh and MacPaint windows. For example, in the last chapter, I often used the Style window to show what option we were discussing. However, I didn't have to actually "draw" any of the windows (well anyway most of them). The way I saved those pictures was by an operation I call "saving the screen." To save any screen image as a MacPaint image, press the ⌘ key, the SHIFT key and the 3 key (at the same time).

158

Try saving the MacPaint screen. Note: If you aren't in MacPaint right now, start it up first, then press the ⌘—SHIFT—3 key combination. You should hear some soft whirring as Mac saves the screen image on the disk. When its done you should see no difference in the screen. So what happened?

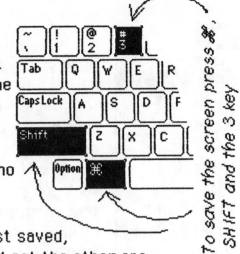

To save the screen press ⌘, SHIFT and the 3 key

To find the screen image we just saved, we'll need to Close this picture and get the other one off of the disk. To do this, point the arrow at the file menu and pull it down until the word Close is highlighted.

Note: An alternate method of Closing a MacPaint document is to click in the small box in the upper left hand corner of the title bar.

File
New
Open...
Close
Save
Save As...
Revert
Print Draft
Print Final
Print Catalog
Quit

One way to Close a MacPaint document is to pull down the File menu until Close is highlighted.

Another way to Close a MacPaint document is to point to the Close box and click in it.

Now pull the File menu down until the word Open... is highlighted. Notice that when we pulled down this menu the first time (on the last page) New and Open... were gray while Close—Print Final were all black. Now, New and Open... are black and Close—Print Final are gray. MacPaint does this to let you know that you cannot Open a file when you have one that is already Open and you cannot Close, or Save a file that is not Open. In other words, MacPaint will not let you try to do anything that is impossible.

Anyway, after you tell MacPaint to Open... a file, you will again hear some whirring and then you will be presented with this file selection window.

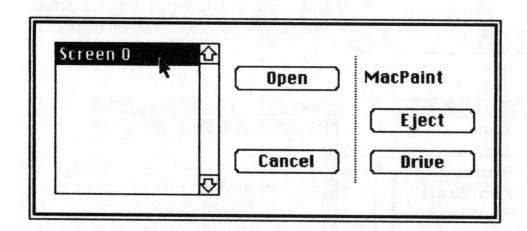

Aha! The screen image was stored for us as a special file that MacPaint called Screen 0. In fact, MacPaint can save any number of screens for us, and each time it does it names that screen "Screen #" (where # is the next higher number available)

so, for example, let's say that you have already got a Screen 0 and a Screen 1 on your disk. The next time you save a screen image, MacPaint will call that screen image Screen 2.

Now, there are two ways that you can Open Screen 0. First, you can select that document by pointing at it and clicking the mouse button once. Then point at the button in the the file selection window labeled Open and press the mouse button again.

Alternately, you can just double-click the word Screen 0. Either way, the disk drive will whirr yet again and this time you will see this in the MacPaint work window:

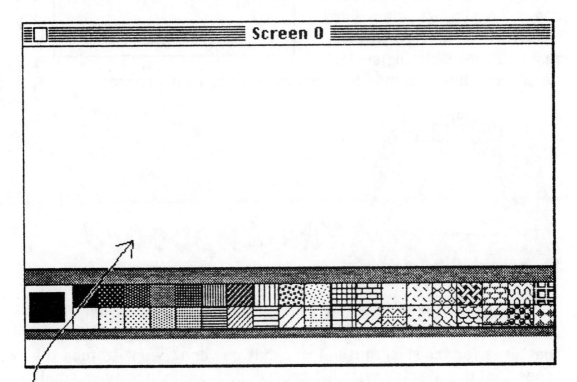

This is a part of the screen that was saved in a MacPaint document called Screen 0. To see more of it, use the Grabber to scroll it into view.

If you look at the picture on the last page, you might think that most of the screen was not saved. Well, in fact, it's all there, but MacPaint cannot fit it all into the work window (obviously, since the work window fits in the screen, it is by necessity, smaller than the screen).

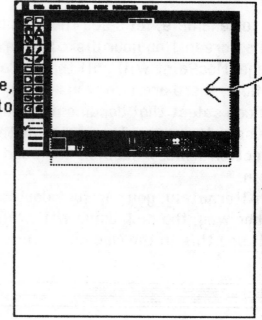

Notice that MacPaint puts the screen image in the upper left-hand corner of the page.

To see the entire screen image as it was stored you can either double-click the Grabber icon 🖑 which will do a Show Page (like the picture on the right). Or you can single-click the Grabber icon and use that to scroll the screen around.

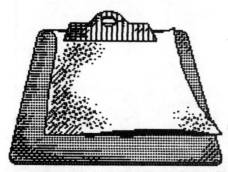

The Clipboard

Okay, now that you've got a picture of the screen, what do you do with it? Well, let's say that you want to make some new patterns for the MacPaint palette, but you don't want to lose the ones that you started with. Of course, you could just make small swatches of all the patterns and save them in a MacPaint file, but by saving a picture of the whole palette you can do this all in just one, simple operation.

Look back at page 161. Recognize the patterns running along the bottom of the screen? That picture is a saved image of the entire palette. Now for our purposes, we don't need to have all of the screen. In fact, all we want to keep is the palette, so use the Grabber (✋) and move the screen around until the whole palette (not including the current pattern window) is visible in the work area.

These are the standard palette patterns

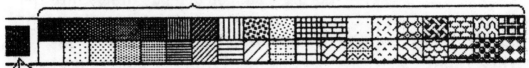

Don't worry about keeping the Current Pattern window in the work area, we'll be removing it anyway.

Once you have the palette centered in the work area, go back to the tool box and get the Selection Box tool (⬚). Use that to select the palette.

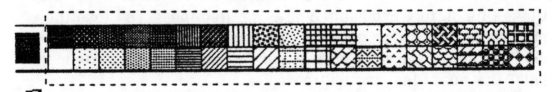

When you select pictures, you can cut off any part of the picture you don't want by simply not selecting that part.

Notice that we selected all of the palette, none of the larger box on the left end of the palette and have allowed sufficient space around the picture to make it easy to align. It is not necessary to position the selection box right up to the picture.

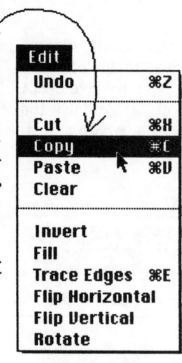

If you have not selected an image, Copy will be gray (inaccessible).

Edit

Undo	⌘Z
Cut	⌘H
Copy	⌘C
Paste	⌘U
Clear	
Invert	
Fill	
Trace Edges	⌘E
Flip Horizontal	
Flip Vertical	
Rotate	

Now point the arrow at the Edit menu and pull it down until the word Copy is highlighted. Note: You can alternatively press the ⌘ key and the "C." This will put the image that you selected into the Clipboard. The Clipboard is used to save images temporarily.

By the way, you can put things into the Clipboard by either Cutting or by Copying (remember, we discussed some of this back in Chapter Two). The difference is when you save to the Clipboard by copying, the picture you are copying from, is not affected. If you save the picture with Cut, the original picture will disappear.

Once you have an image on the Clipboard, you can paste a copy of it anywhere you like. In fact, you can make as many copies of it as you might want. In this case, however, we want to make a new document that will hold an assortment of palettes, so, let's Close this picture and begin a new one. Reminder: To Close the picture you can either double-click the small box in the upper-right corner of the work area or you can pull down the File menu until the word Close is highlighted.

Now all we need to do is Open a new file. Pull down the File menu again, but this time, stop at the word New. This will Open a new picture which MacPaint will temporarily call Untitled (we'll give it a real name later when we save it).

To put the picture that we saved on the Clipboard on the new document, pull down the Edit menu until the word Paste is highlighted. Note: You can alternatively press ⌘ and the "V" key if you don't want to pull down the menu.

164

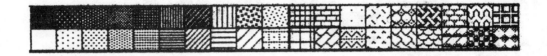

After we have Pasted the image we want onto the new page, all we need to do is clean it up a bit. This is because most of the time we'll pick up some extra bits of lines when we select an image. Now, in this case (as you can see above) we really moved a pretty clean image, but often the pictures wil need some real work.

Big Erasers

Small Erasers

Once we've moved a picture, one of the hardest things to do is clean it up. This usually requires some careful eraser work and, unfortunately, MacPaint has only one size of eraser. However, there are a number of tools that you can use to erase all or parts of your pictures. Which you use will depend on what you are doing, but at least they come in different sizes and shapes.

Using the Paint Brush as an eraser

Look at the picture below. We just finished shading the trunk of the tree, but somehow managed to get "MacPaint" all over the sky. The trouble is, the eraser is so large that we can't really get into the corners around the tree itself without erasing more than we want to erase.

We need to remove the excess shading here

and here

The Eraser will not fit in this area

All we need to do is to select the size and shape eraser we want from among the Paint Brush shapes. Reminder: To select one the of the Paint Brush Shapes, either point at the Goodies menu and pull down to Brush Shape or simply double-click the Paint Brush icon.

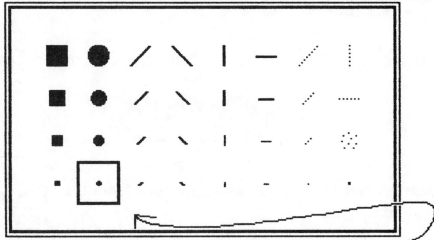

This square shows which Brush Shape has been selected

As you may recall from Chapter One, these are the brush (or in this case eraser) shapes. For our picture, we should probably choose an eraser that is quite small for the smaller areas, however, we will want to use a larger eraser for the wider areas.

To begin with, why don't we choose the small square dot that is usually used with the paint brush (it's marked in the picture above by the square)?

This is a small section of the picture, showing the areas that we want to "clean up". We have selected white for the brush color and as a result we can "paint out" the areas.

Notice how easily the smaller brush fits.

The eraser would be a clumsy tool here.

Big Erasers . . .

Here's an experiment: Select white as the palette pattern.

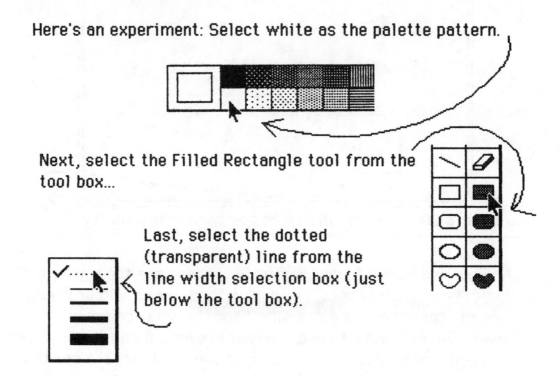

Next, select the Filled Rectangle tool from the tool box...

Last, select the dotted (transparent) line from the line width selection box (just below the tool box).

Now, start in an empty section of the screen and pull down a nice, big rectangle... What? ... Nothing happened ?

Actually something did happen, you just couldn't see it because white against white doesn't show up. But, what you've got now is a dynamically adjustable eraser. It doesn't move as you pull it from one place to another, it just gets bigger in one direction or the other.

Confused? Okay, let's try our eraser trick again, but this time let's actually erase something.

Here's a picture of a can of soup (from the bottom). Unfortunately, the edges of the can got a little messy while it was being ... er... "shaded". Anyway, we need to clean up the sides.

If we try to clean this up with the eraser, it will take a pretty steady hand, but with the white rectangle, we can erase the edges with ease:

Begin in this corner

Note, these dotted lines are just for reference, you would not see them when you use this tool.

This will erase a perfectly straight line along the edge.

As you use this tool, if you find you have erased more than you had intended, just move it back out of the way and the area that disappeared will reappear.

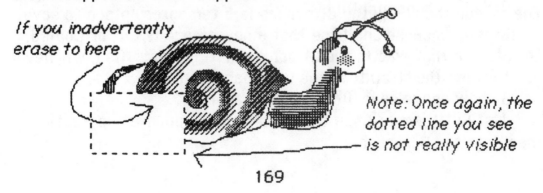

If you inadvertently erase to here

Note: Once again, the dotted line you see is not really visible

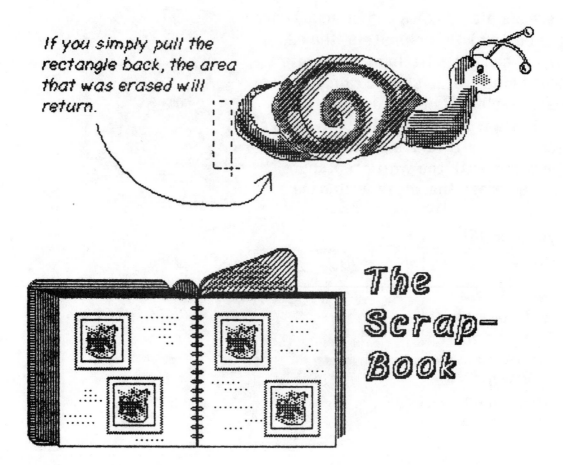

If you simply pull the rectangle back, the area that was erased will return.

The Scrap-Book

Let's take a moment to think about the Clipboard. As you saw earlier, the Clipboard can be used to save pictures temporarily. The reason that I say the Clipboard is a temporary place to save pictures is because any time that a new image is Cut or Copied, the picture that was in the Clipboard will be lost. Also, whenever you turn off the Macintosh the Clipboard is lost.

So how do we save pictures permanently?

Just Cut them or Copy them from the Clipboard and Paste them into the Scrapbook.

170

To use the Scrapbook, pull down the ⌘ menu until the word Scrapbook is highlighted.

Let go of the mouse button and you will hear some soft whirring sounds as the disk drive fetches the pictures that are currently in the Scrapbook. Note: You can Cut, Copy or Paste to the Scrapbook. Also, you can just look through it, just as you might look through any scrapbook.

Anyway, when the disk drive has finally stopped whirring, Mac will display the Scrapbook window as well as the top picture it contains.

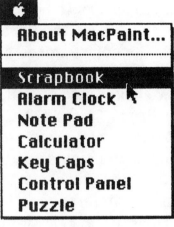

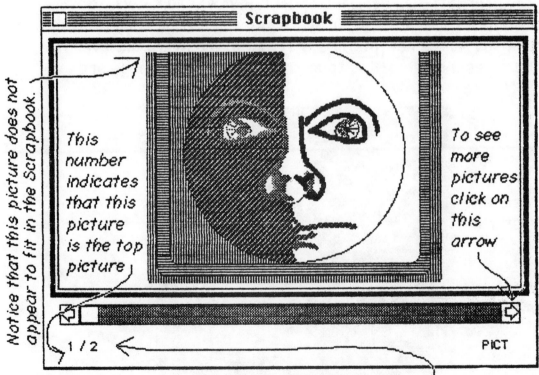

Notice that this picture does not appear to fit in the Scrapbook.

This number indicates that this picture is the top picture

To see more pictures click on this arrow

1 / 2

PICT

This is the number of pictures in the Scrapbook

If you look closely at the picture in the Scrapbook, you'll see that it appears to be "cut off" at both the top and the bottom. This is because the Scrapbook window is not large enough to show the entire image being stored. Note: This does not mean that the picture itself has been cut off. To see the whole picture, all we have to do is Copy it from the Scrapbook - let's do that now. Press ⌘ and the "C" key on the keyboard (or pull down the Edit menu until the word Copy is highlighted).

When the disk drive has stopped whirring (after it has finished puttin the picture into the Clipboard) you will see no apparent difference in the Scrapbook or the Mac screen.

To actually see the image, we'll need to Paste it into a MacPaint document so leave the Scrapbook (click in the small box in upper left-hand corner of the window) and return to MacPaint. Now, clear a space for the picture (if you don't have a blank space, the new picture will be Pasted over whatever is on the screen) by scrolling to an empty spot on the page and press ⌘-P (to Paste).

As you can see, those sections that were hidden in the Scrapbook window were not missing, just covered.

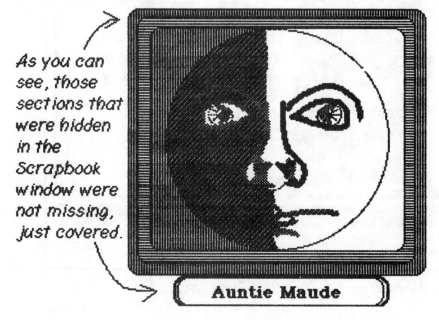

Auntie Maude

172

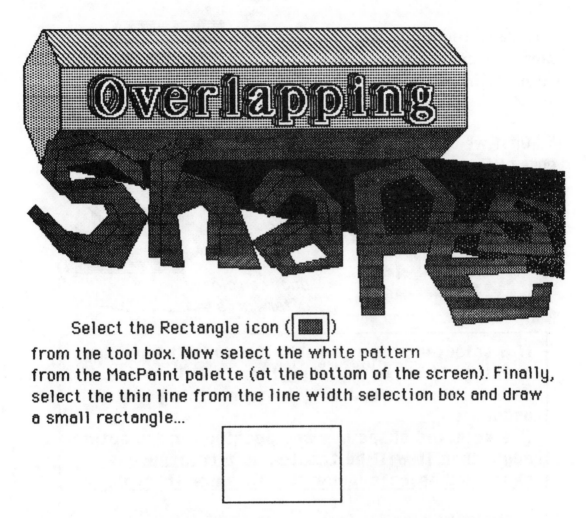

Select the Rectangle icon (▨)
from the tool box. Now select the white pattern
from the MacPaint palette (at the bottom of the screen). Finally,
select the thin line from the line width selection box and draw
a small rectangle...

Now select the rectangle with the lasso, press the Option key on
the keyboard (so you will make a copy of the shape) and move the
copy of the rectangle just slightly down and to the left.

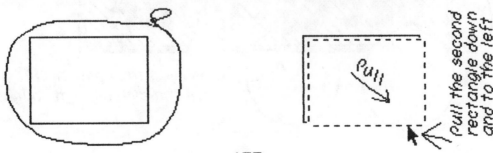

Pull

Pull the second rectangle down and to the left

By repeating this process several times you can produce a stack of cards, each one covering the last.

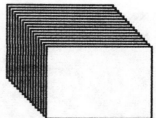

Or if we open just one dot in the edge of the rectangle, we can produce a stack of transparent sheets (of glass?)

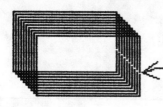

This dot was left open

and then closed afterwards

If a selected shape is solid (i.e. doesn't have any openings in its outer edge),then it will be treated as a solid shape and will cover anything that is under it.

If a selected shape has any openings in its outer edge, then it will be treated as a transparent shape and objects under it will show through.

Notice how the solid circle covers the sign

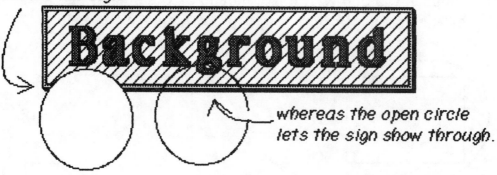

whereas the open circle lets the sign show through.

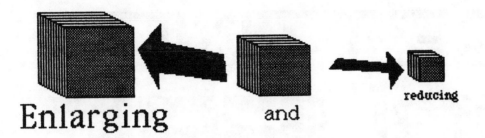

Enlarging and reducing

Enlarging and reducing shapes can be simple or it can be very difficult, however, before we discuss how hard (or easy) it is, we should probably recap the process.

To change the size of an object, you must first select it with the selection box (the lasso will not work). Then, the simplest way to enlarge, reduce or simply change the shape of an object is to press (and hold) the ⌘ key on the keyboard and point the arrow at the object (Note: the tip of the arrow must be inside the selection box. Then simply drag the object to the size and shape you want.

To enlarge the picture, pull the corner of the box away from the center of the picture.

To shrink the picture, drag it in, toward the center of the picture

GETTING SQUARE

Just one last command and then we'll discuss the way that some of the MacPaint features were used to make the pictures in this book. Remember, back in Chapter One, when we talked about the way that the SHIFT key (on the keyboard) can make some of the tools draw straight lines. Well, there's one more thing that it can do. It can make the rectangle tool only draw perfect squares.

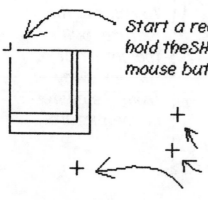

Start a rectangle in this corner (press and hold theSHIFT key before you press the mouse button).

Then try moving the crosshairs in any direction. Regardless of where you move the crosshairs, you'll only get bigger or smaller squares, the sides will all be the same length.

176

MacArt

The next two pages contain an assortment of MacPaint pictures. Look them over before you look at the pages that follow them. Try to figure out how each of the pictures was drawn and which tools were used. If you get stumped, the methods for each of the drawings are in the section after this one.

1.

2.

3.

4.

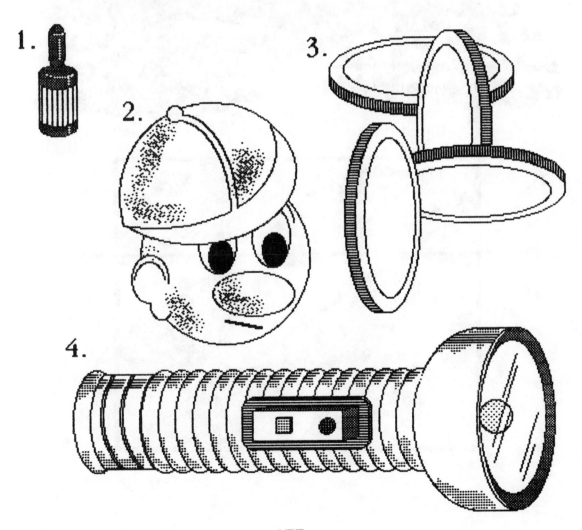

177

5.

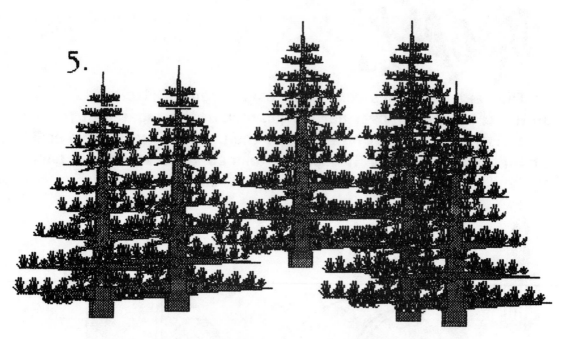

6.

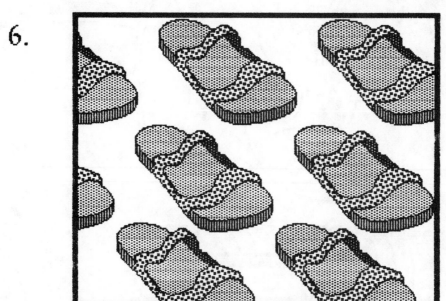

1. The Bottle:

Make a small, horizontal oval: ⟶ ⬭

Lasso the oval to select it.

Press the SHIFT and Option
keys while you pull down a
copy of the oval ⟶

Let go of the SHIFT key and make a third
copy of the oval.

Using the line tool (▱) and the
SHIFT key, connect two of the
ovals together.

Now select the eraser and carefully, erase the
lines inside the bottle.

Make a small, tall oval, using the
rounded rectangle tool and position
it on top of the bottle.
NOTE: It is easier to make the oval
away from the drawing and then select it
with the lasso and "drag" it into position. ⟶

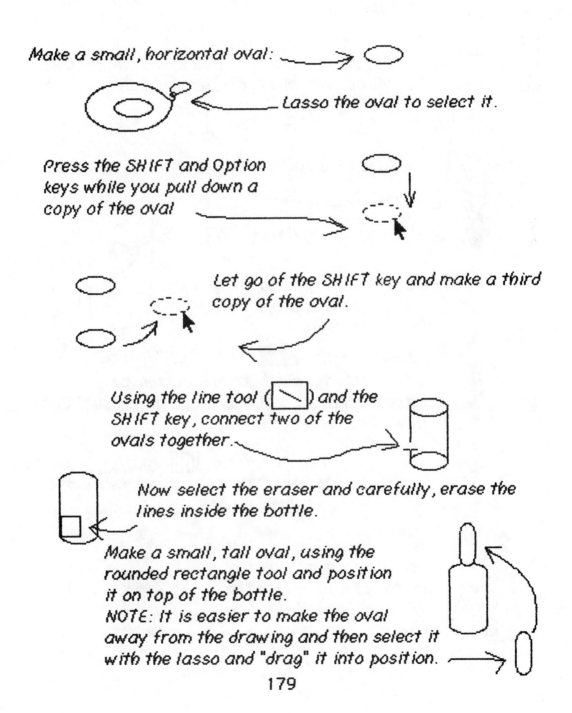

179

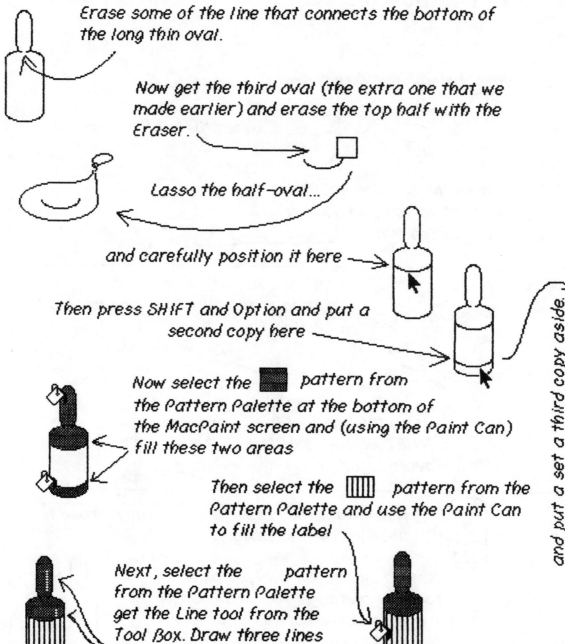

Erase some of the line that connects the bottom of the long thin oval.

Now get the third oval (the extra one that we made earlier) and erase the top half with the Eraser.

Lasso the half-oval...

and carefully position it here →

Then press SHIFT and Option and put a second copy here

and put a set a third copy aside.

Now select the ▪ pattern from the Pattern Palette at the bottom of the MacPaint screen and (using the Paint Can) fill these two areas

Then select the ▐▐▐ pattern from the Pattern Palette and use the Paint Can to fill the label

Next, select the   pattern from the Pattern Palette get the Line tool from the Tool Box. Draw three lines here.

Okay, remember the extra half-oval we made on the last page? ... the one in the margin? Well, go get it now and use the eraser to trim a little bit off of either end of it.

Then use the Lasso to select it and pull down the Edit menu until the word Invert is highlighted. Don't worry if the little crescent seems to disappear – it just turned white...

Put the small white crescent near the top of the bottle

As a final touch, use FatBits to add a highlight to the top of the bottle

and darken the cork...

181

2. The Construction Worker

This drawing is really two drawings in one:
1) The head
2) The hat

To begin the head, select the Circle Tool from the tool box and draw a perfectly round circle about two inches in diameter (don't worry too much about the size—almost any size will do).

Hint: to draw a perfect circle, press and hold the SHIFT key before and while you are drawing the circle.

The construction worker's nose is a small, flat oval.

Note: It is much easier to make the oval away from the face and use the Lasso to move it into position afterwards.

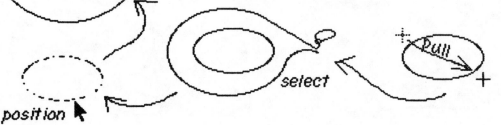

position

select

Pull

The eyes are tall ovals, about the same size as the nose. Since they should both be the same size, we'll just draw one eye and then copy it to make the other.

Draw a small, vertical oval:

and a very small, filled vertical oval:

Now select the small oval with the Lasso and put it inside the larger one.

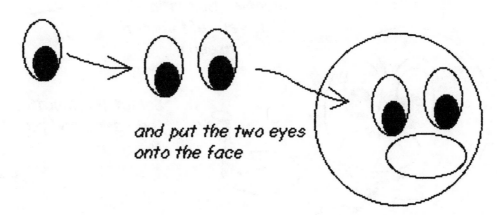

Next, select the eye with the Lasso and make a copy of it...

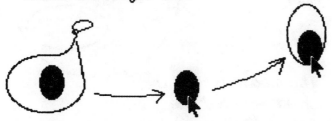

and put the two eyes onto the face

We'll make the eyebrows out of a pair of ovals that are just a bit bigger than the eyes—so draw an oval:

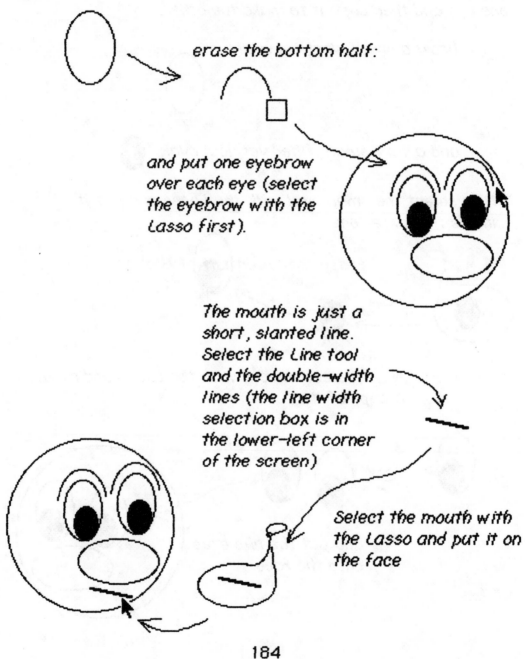

erase the bottom half:

and put one eyebrow over each eye (select the eyebrow with the Lasso first).

The mouth is just a short, slanted line. Select the Line tool and the double-width lines (the line width selection box is in the lower-left corner of the screen)

Select the mouth with the Lasso and put it on the face

All we need to do to complete the face is add an ear. We'll make it out of three small ovals:

#1   #2   #3

To begin with, put oval #2 right below oval #1

and erase the small line between them...

be very careful here

Erase the lower half of oval #3

Select it with the Lasso and put it inside the upper part of the ear.

Next, select the entire ear with the Lasso and put it on the left side of the head...

Note: If the head shows through the ear (like it does on the left) then you have a hole somewhere in the ear. To find the hole, use FatßIts and scroll around the edge of the ear.

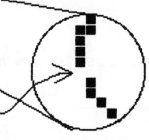

As you can see in this enlargement, there is a hole right here

Okay, now as a finishing touch, erase this line to connect the ear to the head.

Now, the hat: To begin with, draw another circle; but this time you'll need one that is somewhat larger than the circle we made for the head:

Erase part of the circle so you'll be left with a crescent that looks like this.

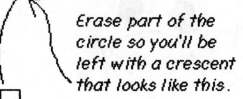

186

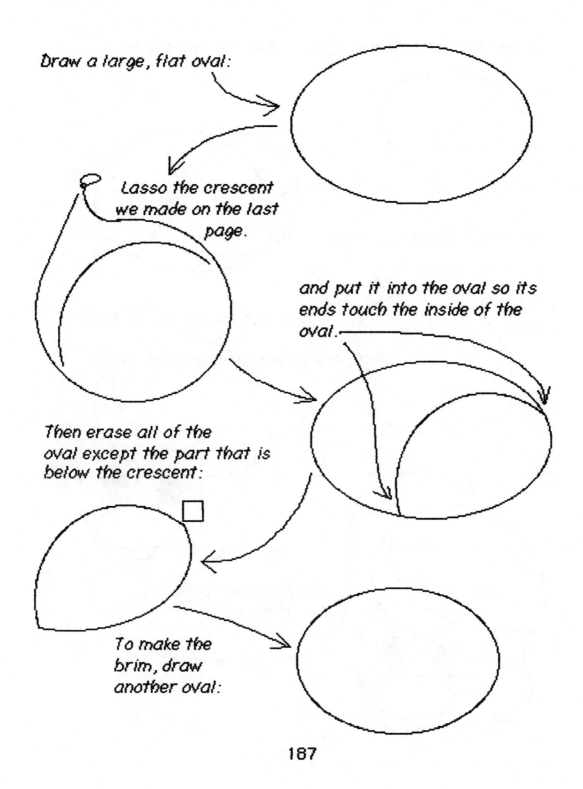

Draw a large, flat oval:

Lasso the crescent we made on the last page.

and put it into the oval so its ends touch the inside of the oval.

Then erase all of the oval except the part that is below the crescent:

To make the brim, draw another oval:

Select the hat with the Lasso and put it on its brim:

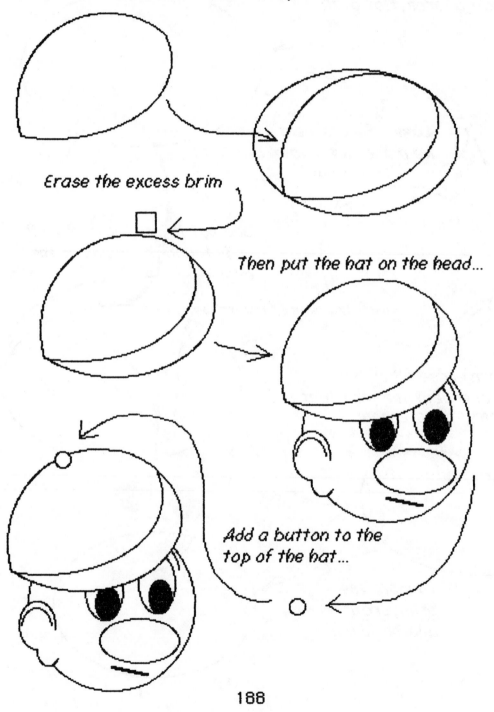

Erase the excess brim

Then put the hat on the head...

Add a button to the top of the hat...

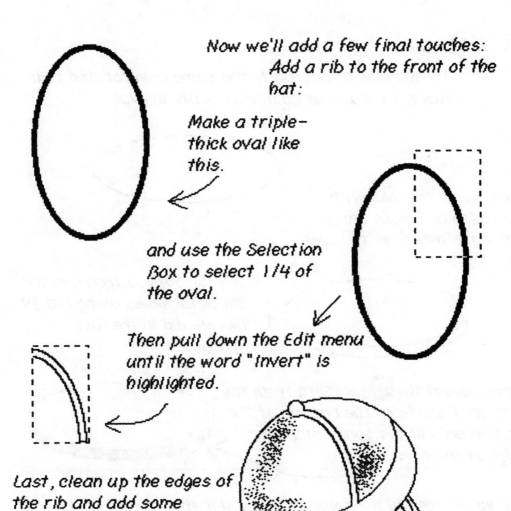

Now we'll add a few final touches: Add a rib to the front of the hat:

Make a triple-thick oval like this.

and use the Selection Box to select 1/4 of the oval.

Then pull down the Edit menu until the word "Invert" is highlighted.

Last, clean up the edges of the rib and add some shading with the spray can.

3. Coins

These coins are actually the same coin rotated four ways. To draw the coin begin with an oval.

Then select the oval with the Lasso and make a copy. Very carefully push the copy up.

↑ *If your copy is transparent, check for holes using FatBit like we did in the last drawing.*

Next, select the 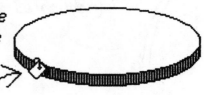 *pattern from the Pattern Palette at the bottom of the screen and fill the space along the edge of the coin.*

Make another oval—somewhat smaller than the first one and position it inside the top of the first.

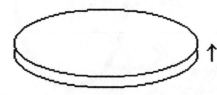

Note: Position the inner oval somewhat closer to the top that the bottom of the outer oval

190

Now all we need to do is make three more copies of the coins, rotated into three different positions:

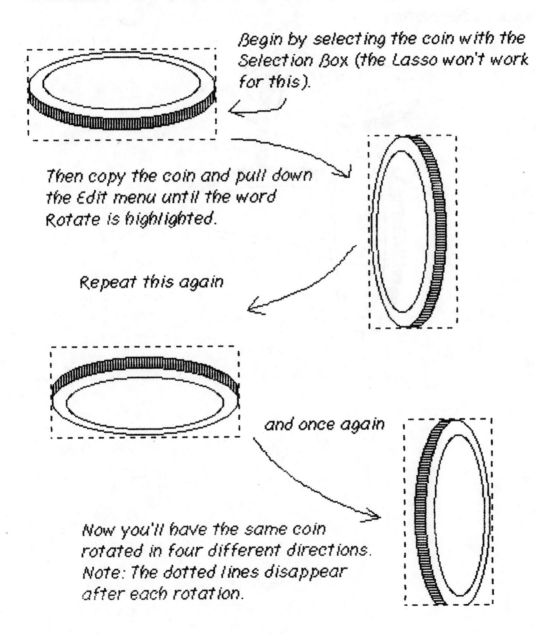

Begin by selecting the coin with the Selection Box (the Lasso won't work for this).

Then copy the coin and pull down the Edit menu until the word Rotate is highlighted.

Repeat this again

and once again

Now you'll have the same coin rotated in four different directions. Note: The dotted lines disappear after each rotation.

191

Now you can use the Lasso to arrange the coins in any way that you like—I recommend overlapping them somewhat to add some depth to the picture.

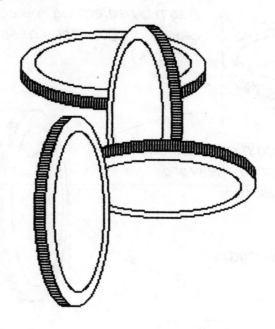

4. Flashlight

The flashlight is made of three major shapes:

> *1) The handle*
> *2) The switch*
> *3) The Reflector*

Let's start with the handle:

> *Draw a tall oval (not too large)*

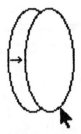

Copy it and move the copy over a bit further than we did the coin. Note: This is to maintain the rounded edges.

Now, here's a trick: We're going to repeat this shape several times to get a ribbed handle. The trouble is, it can be very hard to "eyeball" the alignment of each of the ribs, and we'll want them all to be the same spacing. To eliminate the possiblity of any misalignment, click the mouse button once to deselect the first oval and reselect the double oval.

To get alignment correct press the SHIFT key and the Option key. Then move the oval pair to the right one oval width. When the left oval is exactly over the right oval they will blend into one shape. Stop there, let go of the mouse button and press it again to make the next copy.

Using the method described on the last page, make the handle sixteen segments long:

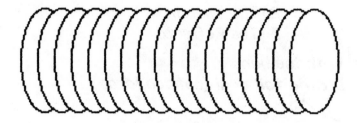

Now, the rear section of the flashlight has screw-on threads but only has one rib—at the rear. To draw the cap, make another ribbed section four ribs long.

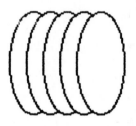

Draw a horizontal line along the top and bottom like this:

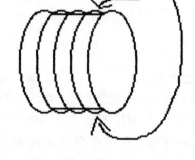

and erase all of the inside lines and the ribs:

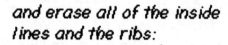

Next, draw an oval that's a bit taller and wider than the ribs.

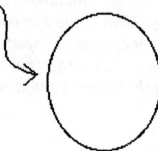

194

Using the eraser, erase all of the oval except a section large enough to fit inside the barrel of the cap. Note: Leave a section that as just a bit off-center so the threads will appear to spiral.

Now, Lasso the section of oval and position it inside the barrel like this:

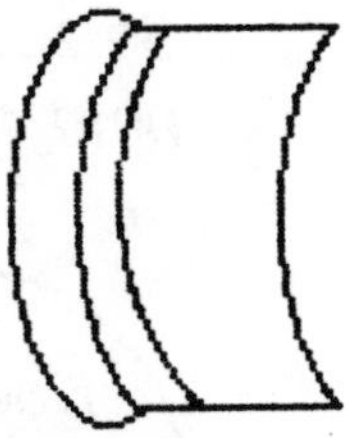

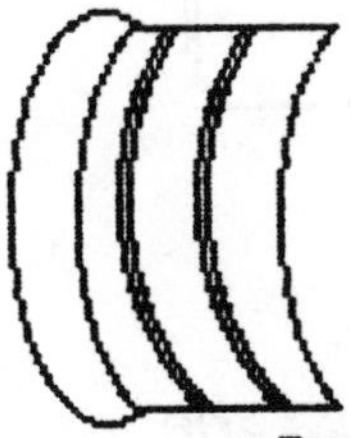

Keep on selecting the oval section and (using the SHIFT and Option keys) make two lines, close together and another pair of lines away from the first ones (also close together).

Now select the cap with the Lasso and join it to the handle.

Leave one-line gap here to darken the joint between the cap and handle.

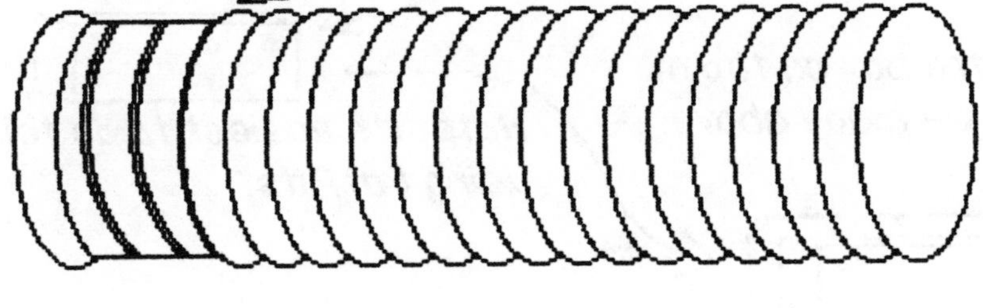

Next, we'll make the switch:

Use the Rounded Rectangle too and make a medium-sized rectangle:

Select it with the Lasso and make a second copy right next to it to give the shape some depth.

Now draw a square-edged rectangle (using the Rectangle tool).

Make a copy of this too, but make the copy much further over than the last one:

Now join the corners with some short lines:

and erase the lines inside the corners:

Now put the box on top of the plate we made above.

Note: Its easiest to do this using FatBits.

Okay, let's add a couple buttons to the switch:
(One will be round and the other will be square):
Draw a small circle and a small square:

Select them with the Lasso and make copies
as we did before, to give them depth:

Position them on the switch:

and put the switch on the handle:

The last part of the flashlight we'll need to make is the
reflector. Begin by making a large oval:

This will become the body of
the reflector.

197

Now, follow this section carefully, the next part is a little tricky:

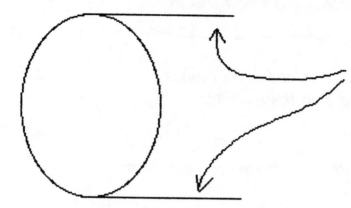

Draw horizontal, straight lines (use the SHIFT key) that connect to the top and bottom of the oval.

Then get the Oval tool again and put the cross hair on the top line (about three inches to the right of the oval). Then draw an oval by pulling the cross hair down to the bottom line and over just enough to make a narrow oval.

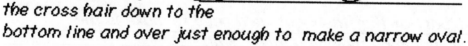

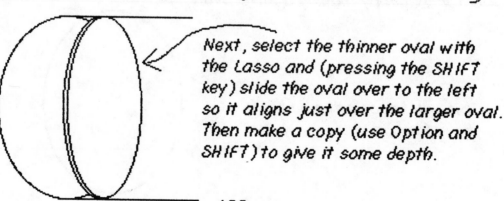

Next, select the thinner oval with the Lasso and (pressing the SHIFT key) slide the oval over to the left so it aligns just over the larger oval. Then make a copy (use Option and SHIFT) to give it some depth.

198

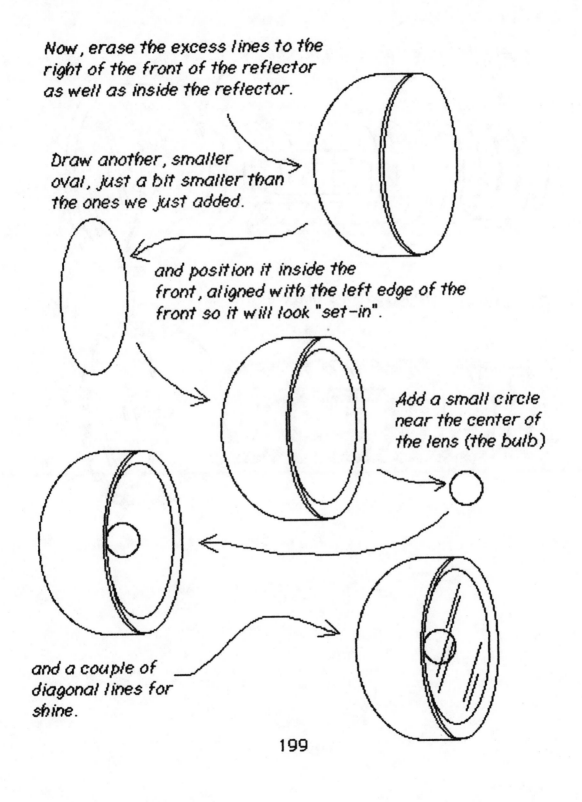

Now, erase the excess lines to the right of the front of the reflector as well as inside the reflector.

Draw another, smaller oval, just a bit smaller than the ones we just added.

and position it inside the front, aligned with the left edge of the front so it will look "set-in".

Add a small circle near the center of the lens (the bulb)

and a couple of diagonal lines for shine.

199

Now join the reflector to the handle:

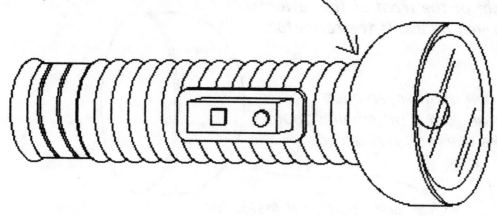

Add a few finishing touches and we're done!

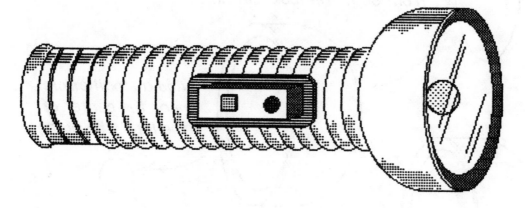

5. Pine Trees

The pine trees consist of two very simple shapes: The trunks and the needles (or branches).

A pine tree trunk looks like a tall triangle. To draw it, get the Connected Line tool from the tool box and select the narrowest line width (not the dotted line).

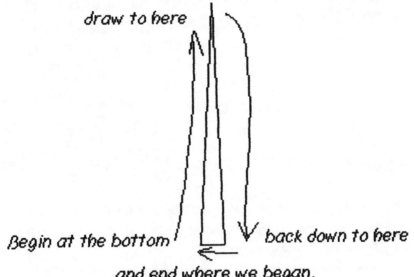

draw to here

Begin at the bottom *back down to here*

and end where we began.

Now select the ▓ pattern from the Pattern Palette. Then get the Paint Can and fill the tree trunk with the gray pattern.

The branches are very similar to the trunk except they are horizontal and (of course) much smaller.

Make several branches in different sizes:

201

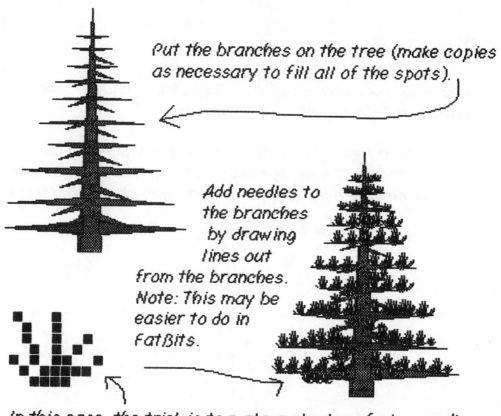

Put the branches on the tree (make copies as necessary to fill all of the spots).

Add needles to the branches by drawing lines out from the branches. Note: This may be easier to do in FatBits.

In this case, the trick is to make a cluster of pine needles and then use the Lasso to select the cluster. Then copy them along each of the branches.

Put several trees together and you've got a forest!

6. Big, Repeating Patterns

As you probably recall from the section on making your own patterns (in Chapter One), the pattern in the MacPaint Palette are limited to 64 dots (an 8x8 pattern). While it is possible to do quite a bit with this, there are occasions when 8x8 is just too small.

Because MacPaint has the ability to repeat anything it can produce, we can actually use any drawing as a pattern if we are willing to repeat it manually.

Here, we'll learn how to repeat the patterns with some ease and flexibility.

For example, here is a large shape (you can use any shape you like). Now, to repeat this shape, just select it with the Lasso, press the Option key and pull a copy off of the original. We have done this before.

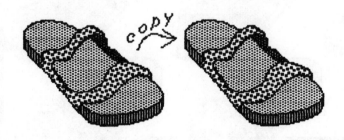

Next, select the two shapes together (using the Lasso) and make another copy below the two originals.

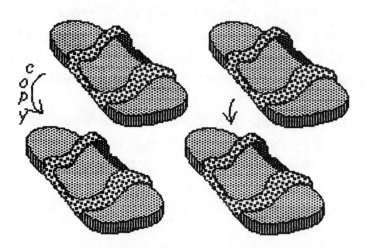

Keep copying the shapes (aligning them as you go) until you have enough to fill the frame you want, then use the Rectangle tool to surround your pattern.

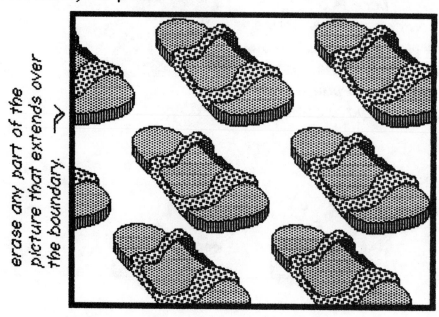

erase any part of the picture that extends over the boundary.

The End...

Well, that's about it, you now know what MacPaint can do. As you can see from the previous examples, drawing pictures with MacPaint is mostly a matter of putting different shapes together.

Although there really isn't much I say about MacPaint that I haven't already said, I would like to leave you with one parting idea...

Enter this exactly as shown:

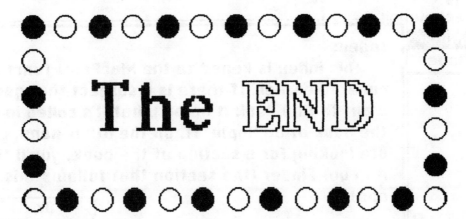

Now, select the whole thing with the Lasso and Invert it (you know, pull down the Edit menu to the word Invert). Then, move the Lasso out of the way and click the mouse button.

Now you'll have an inverted image of the original—right? Okay, but now press and hold the ⌘ key and the "Z" key on the keyboard.

INDEX

Contents

Introduction

The Toolbox
Edit
Goodies
Font
FontSize
Style
Techniques
Index
Finder

Index:

   This index is keyed to the MacPaint functions covered earlier. If there is a subject that you want to find, look it up by what it's called in the book or by Apple. If, on the other hand, you are looking for a section of the book, you'll find it in our Finder (the section that follows this one).

[OK]

FINDER

Finder:

    Do not confuse this Finder with the one that Macintosh uses to locate things on the Desk top. This Finder helps you to "find" things in the MacPaint Notebook. You'll find every Chapter, section, and sub-section listed in order and by name, so if you want to find a subject that you read in here, use this finder.

OK

211